A CASEBOOK FOR
STUDENT LEADERS

A CASEBOOK FOR STUDENT LEADERS

Robert Holkeboer
Eastern Michigan University

Thomas Hoeksema
New Mexico State University

HOUGHTON MIFFLIN COMPANY   Boston   New York

Director of Student Success Programs: Barbara A. Heinssen
Associate Editor: Melissa Plumb
Associate Project Editor: Tamela Ambush
Editorial Assistant: Jodi O'Rourke
Senior Production/Design Coordinator: Sarah Ambrose
Manufacturing Manager: Florence Cadran

Cover Design: Rebecca Fagan

The cases are based on real events but names and circumstances have been
changed to protect the identities of the individuals and institutions involved.

Printed in the U.S.A.

Library of Congress Catalog Card Number: 97-72487

Student Book ISBN: 0-395-85704-X

123456789-DSG-01 00 99 98 97

Contents

PART ONE
Leadership and Values   1

CASE ONE
The Thief Who Got Robbed   3

> Senator Joe Biden did it in a speech. Martin Luther King, Jr. did it
> in his doctoral dissertation. Just how serious a crime is plagiarism, and
> why do faculty go ballistic when college students commit it? You be
> the judge.

CASE TWO
The Midnight Hacker   9

> How do you tell your best friend he's a thief?

CASE THREE
A Crisis of Conscience   13

> After four years in college, Tad had grown accustomed to adminis-
> trative foul-ups—usually billing errors in the college's favor. But this
> one was different—a one-way ticket to one of the best law schools in
> the country!

CASE FOUR
The Mind of the Beholder 47

Is it art or pornography? Adam thinks it's art, but a wealthy benefactor disagrees. Who will win the argument?

CASE FIVE
The Loneliness of the Long-Distance Runner 51

Gender equity, mandated for all member conferences of the NCAA, was a major breakthrough for female student athletes. But Doug is feeling the pinch.

CASE SIX
The Coach Who Talked Trash 55

The coach was a master of words. His locker room speeches at halftime were legendary. Then one day he used the wrong word, and suddenly it was all over.

PART THREE
Leadership and Diversity 59

CASE ONE
Logomania 61

Fairfax State's new president alters a cherished nickname, and the campus is in an uproar.

CASE TWO
The Skinhead 67

He shaves his head and wears a safety pin in his nose. Does that make him a criminal?

CASE THREE
The Price of Compassion 73

According to the Americans with Disabilities Act, colleges are obligated to make a "reasonable effort" to accommodate people with special needs. But isn't Edna being a little unreasonable?

To the Facilitator

A Casebook for Student Leaders is intended for a broad audience of college students, some of whom already occupy positions of responsibility on campus and others who have not yet taken an active part in the leadership process. Our assumptions are that

- leadership is a process that creates change;
- the change-making process requires both leaders and followers;
- leaders and followers need each other.

A Casebook for Student Leaders is designed to help students acquire the skills needed for the leadership process to work—skills that will be essential to their survival in the professional job market they are about to enter. These skills—written and oral communication, critical thinking and problem solving, and teamwork—are learnable and accessible to all, not just the "born leader."

Case learning is a powerful method for teaching these survival skills. It is experiential, interactive, and enjoyable. It really works.

PURPOSE AND DESIGN

A Casebook for Student Leaders can be used as a stand-alone or secondary text in a variety of college classroom settings or as a training manual in workshops, conferences, leadership training seminars, and retreats. Each of the cases will provoke animated discussion, causing students to become more aware of leadership dynamics while challenging them to find and assert a personal leadership style that is authentic and effective. The text provides a lively alternative or supplement to leadership theory, while reinforcing the fundamental knowledge and guiding principles taught in management and leadership training courses. Because case learning is by nature interactive, the text also works well in introductory interpersonal and small-group communication courses. And its abundance of purposeful writing exercises are well suited to intermediate and advanced courses in written communication.

STRUCTURE AND RECURRING FEATURES

A Casebook for Student Leaders addresses consequential and timely issues that reflect the contemporary college environment. Students respond with lively interest to these cases, which are rooted in their own academic culture and which reflect the realities and eccentricities of higher education in the 1990s.

Twenty-four cases—all based on actual situations—are presented. Six cases are grouped under each of four general headings:

- Leadership and Values
- Leadership and Individual Rights
- Leadership and Diversity
- Leadership and Group Dynamics

Each of the twenty-four cases is accompanied by six activities, each requiring a different learning strategy.

1. *Questions to Guide Discussion* immediately follows each case. These open-ended questions enable students, working in small groups, to begin the process of "unpacking the case."

2. *Now What If?* is a case-enrichment exercise that invites students to consider alternative case scenarios and their implications. These scenarios are especially useful when there is a "rush to judgment" or when a discussion stalls.

3. *Case in Point* extends the discussion of the case to some dimension of leadership principles, research, or theory and includes an exercise that can be done alone or collaboratively.

4. *Writing Assignment* may be assigned at the facilitator's discretion. These assignments are short, purposeful writing tasks calling for a wide variety of strategies, styles, and audiences. They allow students to explore the cases in greater depth.

5. *Showtime* is a role-playing or presentational activity that is both instructive and fun. This activity is an opportunity for students to develop their communication and leadership skills and to express, empathize with, and respond to differing viewpoints.

6. *Research Kit* encourages students to conduct background research by identifying and locating primary source materials and interviewing experts. To get them started, the kit at the end of each case lists (1) print and on-line resources and (2) human resources. Because procedural, political, ethical, and legal issues are almost always inseparable, the kits often in-

clude attorneys' names, conduct codes, policy manuals, and legal documents. Students with access to the Internet will enjoy locating and downloading many of the print resources from the World Wide Web and discovering hundreds of new and interesting web sites in the process.

At the end of the text is the *Selected Bibliography*—an extensive listing of reference works, books, articles, and Internet resources grouped under six broad topics:

- Leadership Studies
- Teaching and Learning with Cases
- Conflict Resolution
- Group Discussion and Team Building
- Critical Thinking
- Useful Internet Resources

The works cited were selected for their practical value in college-level case-learning and leadership training settings.

THE CASE APPROACH TO LEARNING

The case method is a time-tested, collaborative, diagnostic learning strategy. Students work together to solve a case in much the same way a team of surgeons works together to diagnose a patient's symptoms. A case is simply a story whose ending is written by the reader. In this respect, it resembles a story problem in mathematics. Some have called case learning a half-finished chess game: a problem presents itself, along with many possible solutions. By using a systematic critical-thinking process, students learn to discard solutions that offer short-term gains and easy answers and to identify those that promise the most favorable outcome for the greatest number of people.

The Three-Step Process.   Typically, students work through each case in small groups, guided by a three-step critical-thinking process.

1. Identify the core problem.
2. Brainstorm possible solutions.
3. Agree on the best solution.

This small-group discussion process normally takes at least twenty minutes. The entire class then meets in plenary session as individual group leaders report on their groups' deliberations and, with the facilitator's guidance, further refine the case solution.

Case learning is characterized by lively discussion and group interaction. Students learn pleasurably because they are working in a social setting to solve problems that bear directly on their lives. The case method helps students to internalize learning derived from textbooks, lectures, and authorities.

A Casebook for Student Leaders engages college students in a range of timely and significant issues that reflect the realities of their college environment. Each case poses a complex problem that requires thorough and rigorous analysis. Controversial issues such as intercultural conflict, sexual assault, and academic integrity are embedded in a critical situation in which all of the issue's ambiguities, tensions, and argumentative strategies come into sharp focus.

Through their encounters with the issues and with each other, students gain experience in making constructive and appropriate contributions in a group or committee setting. By grappling with cases rooted in familiar contexts, they learn how to develop, demonstrate, express, and analyze traits of effective leadership. Through facilitated small-group discussions, they arrive at workable and ethically coherent positions on such difficult issues as individual freedom and social responsibility, multicultural sensitivity, relationships with faculty and work supervisors, gender roles, balancing academic responsibilities with the need for personal growth, and personal values.

Existing texts on leadership tend to be theoretical. They teach what leadership *is* but offer little practice in the skills that leadership *requires*. These skills include the following:

- Thinking creatively and critically about a complex problem
- Communicating effectively with individuals and groups
- Mobilizing support for an idea
- Working toward consensus as a member of a team
- Valuing diverse points of view
- Communicating forcefully and persuasively about real issues
- Knowing when to act alone

It is precisely these skills that *A Casebook for Student Leaders* is designed to teach.

FACILITATOR SUPPORT

As facilitators guide students through the cases, they will acquire skills of their own in basic case-facilitation techniques: asking discovery questions, shifting viewpoints, encouraging disagreement, dealing with unplanned silences, moving from solution to application, and introducing overlooked topics. The facilitators' challenge is to help students solve problems, make decisions, assign priorities, resolve conflicts, build consensus, and think intensely and systematically. Ultimately, they are responsible for stimulating, redirecting, and enriching the group discussion, while avoiding the temptation to control it.

To assist instructors and group leaders, a special *Facilitator's Manual* is available. This manual, rich with practical and substantive advice, is an indispensable guide to the case-learning process. It contains background information, classroom-tested techniques, and case-by-case instructions that result in lively, purposeful small-group discussions and satisfying case solutions.

Section I of the manual ("Recurring Features of the Text") explains when and how to integrate the text features (*Case, Questions to Guide Discussion, Now What If?, Case in Point, Writing Assignment, Showtime, Research Kit,* and *Selected Bibliography*) in a class, workshop, or seminar. This section equips facilitators with the tools needed to develop a responsive, collaborative, and learner-centered environment.

Section II ("Case-by-Case Analysis") is a substantive case-by-case guide that examines each of the twenty-four cases in relation to the recurring features discussed in Section I of the manual. Section II concludes with "The Leadership Issue," which identifies and enlarges upon the leadership questions at the heart of each case.

Section III ("The Art of Case Learning: Facilitation Techniques") provides the instructor or group leader with suggestions, techniques, and information about facilitating small-group discussions and being an effective case leader. Case leaders are taken step by step through various facilitation strategies, given guidelines on how to reach consensus through collaboration, and provided with practical methodologies for resolving conflicts. The goal of this section is to help facilitators promote analytical group interaction, develop a broad range of alternative responses, stimulate new ways of thinking about complex issues, and encourage leadership skills through a student-centered form of instruction.

Educators at all levels face unique challenges as they attempt to empower students with the skills demanded by the twenty-first-century workplace. *A Casebook for Student Leaders* provides an innovative, interactive format in which students can define leadership in relation to the rapidly changing world they inhabit, while at the same time developing the expertise and sensitivity that the world will demand of them as tomorrow's leaders.

ACKNOWLEDGMENTS

Like the leadership process itself, the writing, editing, and manufacture of a text like this one involves many important contributors besides the authors. We would like to thank the following people—students, educators, reviewers, and the outstanding editorial and production staff at Houghton Mifflin—for their invaluable help. From Eastern Michigan University, Jennifer Beller,

xvi   TO THE FACILITATOR

Margie Brooks, Deborah Dezure, Janice Habarth, Colonel David Klubeck, and Anne McKee; from SUNY–Buffalo, Mary H. Gresham; from Pennsylvania State University, Christine Phelps; from New Mexico State University, John Loveland and Bob Smiggen, and the focus group of honors students and student leaders; John Fuller from Fountain Valley School in Colorado Springs and Tim Monroe from Las Cruces High School; Janice Beran, McLennan Community College, Texas; Peter Eckel, American Council on Education (Washington, D.C.); Julie Grinolds, Lewis-Clark State College (ID); Brenda Morris, Baylor University, Texas; Alexandra Jepson Rodgers, Florida State University; Kathy M. Shellogg, St. Norbert College, Wisconsin; Janice Sheppard, University of Wisconsin—Madison; Susan S. Tully, Aiken Technical College (SC); Pamela M. Tyahur, Miami University of Ohio; and the fine student leaders from Eastern Michigan University and New Mexico State University.

Our incomparable editor at Houghton Mifflin, Melissa Plumb, and former Student Success Programs director, Bill Webber, deserve major credit for this book, but they would want to share it with their editorial and production staff: Tamela Ambush, Jodi O'Rourke, Sarah Ambrose, and Florence Cadran.

Despite the painstaking effort of so many people to rid the text of errors, some faults have nevertheless remained. These are the inescapable responsibility of the authors.

R. H.
T. H.

To the Student

WHAT IS LEADERSHIP?

Some people think that leadership is a rare and innate gift, something only a few people are born with. Others believe it is a skill that can be acquired with patient effort. Both views contain a measure of truth: strong leaders make the most of their native ability by hard work.

Leadership may be defined as a group process designed to bring about change. Although anyone can take part in the leadership process, their effectiveness will increase to the extent that they develop the skills emphasized throughout this text: critical thinking and problem solving, written and oral communication, and teamwork. They are skills that anyone can learn, and you'll be improving them as you and your classmates work through the cases in this text.

The twenty-four cases are arranged around four broad themes:

- Leadership and Values
- Leadership and Individual Rights
- Leadership and Diversity
- Leadership and Group Dynamics

Tomorrow's leaders must have a strong value system authenticated by their own experience; an understanding of how individual rights sometimes clash with social responsibility; an appreciation of the value of diverse cultures; an empathy for divergent viewpoints; and an intuitive understanding of human behavior and group dynamics.

WHAT IS CRITICAL THINKING?

When faced with two alternatives—one clearly less attractive than the other—we can rely on our common sense to make the better choice. But the really difficult problems in life have many possible solutions. They tug at our values and force us to weigh one value against another. Critical thinking can be defined as "uncommon sense"—a higher order of thinking that allows us to sort through a host of choices, narrow them down to a few good ones, and then pick the best one.

Let's consider an extreme example of a difficult moral situation in which people were forced to do something they believed was morally wrong to bring about a greater good. During the German occupation of the Netherlands in World War II, the Dutch underground saved a few Jews from the death camps by hiding them in people's homes. Many of the Dutch civilians who sheltered Jews at the risk of their own lives were devout, God-fearing Calvinists. When the Gestapo knocked on their door and asked if they were hiding Jews, they were forced to choose between their commitment to protect their Jewish friends and their obedience to the biblical commandment "Thou shalt not bear false witness." To tell the truth would have meant certain death to their Jewish friends; to lie, from their religious perspective, meant their own spiritual death.

Many of the great issues of our time appear to offer only two alternatives or to pit one great value against another. Capital punishment, for example, stirs heated controversy because it appears to force a choice between mercy and justice. The abortion issue has been framed as a debate between two rights—life and choice. Some argue that affirmative action obliges people to choose between fairness to one group and unfairness to another.

In reality, however, the serious dilemmas we encounter in life, and the ones you will encounter in this book, have many possible solutions. Most of the dilemmas in this text have lower stakes than capital punishment, abortion, or affirmative action, but they are no less complex and ambiguous. There is no right answer, no perfect solution, although some solutions are better than others. Critical thinking is a systematic way of finding the best solution.

It's not an easy task. Critical thinking is hard work. But it's a skill that most humans are born with and one that can be developed with practice.

CRITICAL THINKING AND
THE CASE-LEARNING PROCESS

Here is the basic three-step critical-thinking process you'll be using as you work through the cases.

Step 1   IDENTIFY THE CORE PROBLEM

Faced with a difficult crisis and paralyzed by fear, people are often unable to identify the core problem they face. And if you can't identify it, you can't solve it. Leaders have the ability to remain cool in a crisis, do a quick situation analysis, and ask the important questions: What is the *real* problem here?

What aspects of the problem are less significant and less urgent? What needs to be done *right away?*

Identifying the core problem is often a matter of values and priorities. To pretest your own critical-thinking ability, read carefully the following situation and then answer the questions at the end:

> *Dana has just begun her first real job as a counselor at a summer camp for girls. She is responsible for twelve 13-year-old girls. One of the girls, Sasha, has been acting strangely. Sullen and withdrawn, she rarely shows up for meals and is reluctant to participate in camp activities. Sasha's best friend, Carrie, mentions to Dana that Sasha has been talking about killing herself. Dana is alarmed and asks Carrie to keep an eye on Sasha at all times. Carrie agrees.*
>
> *One afternoon, while Dana is teaching archery, a camper rushes up and tells Dana that Sasha is missing and there are open containers of pills on her bedside table. Dana turns to Carrie and snaps, "Why weren't you there? I told you to keep an eye on Sasha! We're going to have a talk, young lady!" Dana then takes Carrie to the camp office and gives her a stern lecture about the importance of responsibility.*

QUESTIONS

1. What is the core problem that needs to be dealt with right away?
2. What is the core problem from Dana's point of view?
3. What values require that Dana get help for Sasha? What values require that Carrie be disciplined?
4. What may have caused Dana to make a bad decision in this instance?

Step 2   BRAINSTORM POSSIBLE SOLUTIONS

Good chess players have the ability simultaneously to consider both the many possible moves of their opponent and their own response to each of those moves. This requires imagination—an essential trait of leaders and one that all humans possess in varying degrees. The advantage of solving problems in a group is that some people will see possibilities that others miss. Together, you can brainstorm a fairly complete list of possible solutions to a case.

Brainstorming requires that everyone be allowed to put anything on the table, no matter how silly, without fear of being put down by other members of the group. In the case above, Dana's actions represent one possible solution to the case. What other solutions can you think of? Write them down fairly quickly, without censoring yourself; then share them with your small group. Each group member should share at least one solution.

Although it's OK to ask for clarification of an idea, don't evaluate the suggestions at this stage—you'll be doing that in Step 3. Just say any possible course of action that comes to mind. A volunteer should write all the ideas in abbreviated form on poster paper or a chalkboard. They should be written large enough for everyone to read.

Step 3   CHOOSE THE BEST SOLUTION

Once everyone's ideas are on the table, you can examine them carefully. Which ones seem like good ideas? What makes a solution a good one? The one that's easiest? Safest? Just any solution that solves the main character's problem? Which solutions are least appealing? Why? As you work through the cases, you'll be developing your own criteria for what constitutes a good solution. In the process, you'll be clarifying and strengthening your personal values—another trait of the successful leader.

One good way to evaluate possible solutions is to make a list of desired outcomes of the case. Which solution achieves most, if not all, of the desired outcomes?

Another way is to turn the problem inside out: If a bad situation looks like this, what would a good situation look like? The negative aspects of the current situation turned into their opposites can become the desired outcomes.

Another good test is to ask the question, Which solution offers the best outcome for all affected parties—the greatest good for the greatest number?

A favorable outcome should be stated positively rather than negatively. In the case above, for example, a negative solution might look like this:

Sasha doesn't commit suicide.

Dana doesn't focus on Carrie.

Carrie doesn't get punished for leaving Sasha.

A positive outcome could be stated like this:

Sasha gets a better understanding of her problems and adopts a more positive outlook on life.

Dana makes sure Sasha is OK and gets her the help she needs.

In general, you should try to reach agreement in your group on what you think is the best solution. Since your time for discussion will be limited and many different value systems will be present in your group, reaching a consensus will often be difficult and sometimes impossible. The process of collaboration will test your effectiveness as a leader. When should you give in, and when should you stick to your guns? You also will have an opportunity to develop skills in conflict management—helping others to resolve their differences, learning to respect people even when they hold opposing views, learning to disagree and still respect each other—all traits of effective leaders.

OTHER LEADERSHIP SKILLS

As you work through the cases with your peers, you will be learning not only to speak but also to listen. A characteristic of effective leaders is their ability to listen and respond appropriately. Leaders require many things, but they are nothing without followers. In a democratic society, it is both impossible and undesirable to lead people in a direction they do not want to go. For this reason, leaders must be effective communicators. And communication requires, far more than speaking ability, the ability to listen to others. Students whose leadership skills consist of nothing more than a loud voice and an aggressive, domineering manner will soon discover the ineffectiveness of these traits in case discussions.

Although we have been emphasizing critical-thinking and communication skills here, there are, of course, many other leadership skills worth cultivating: the courage to express an unpopular point of view or to admit you were wrong in front of others; the humility to take responsibility for a mundane but necessary chore that no one else is willing to take on; and compassion and sensitivity to members of your group who are being ignored or feeling left out.

Leadership is a group process in which everyone has something to contribute. During a discussion, the role of leader often shifts from one person to another. Every member of the team has something worthwhile to contribute. Some leaders are rabble-rousers. Others seem always to play the role of sand in the oyster or devil's advocate. Some are quiet and studious, speaking rarely; when they do speak, everyone listens because they are so often right. Still others are painstaking and conscientious, doing the grunt work and cleaning up the mess after everyone else has left. Sometimes leaders emerge as a beacon in the darkness—acting alone, under pressure, with little or no support, setting an example for others simply by doing the right thing.

Different situations require different types of leaders. You never know when it will be your turn to step forward and be counted. Will you be ready?

A CASEBOOK FOR
STUDENT LEADERS

Leadership and Values

The process of clarifying values—fine-tuning our view of what is good or evil, true or false, ugly or beautiful—is at its most intense during college. Student leaders have an obligation to clarify and strengthen their values by carefully considering the consequences of the various courses of action available to them. And they need to understand the law, which is based on societal values. The values of strong leaders are a source of courage to them in situations that are full of risk. Weak values are fatal because they fail to sustain the leader in times of crisis.

The Thief Who Got Robbed

As chair of the Student Judiciary Committee, Winnie has just heard the evidence in a plagiarism case. Ingrid, the student who has been accused, is no academic slouch struggling to get by, but a senior English major and Rhodes scholar nominee with a 3.9 grade point average (GPA). She has been accused by her instructor of copying portions of a published article almost verbatim and passing it off as her own work. The instructor has created transparencies showing the article and the paper side by side to support the charge of plagiarism.

In her defense, Ingrid has argued that the plagiarism was not intentional but that, because she was extremely busy, she neglected to document her source as carefully as she should have. (The paper does include some footnoted quotations from the original work.)

The director of the Honors Program has testified to Ingrid's high character and extraordinary ability and to the countless hours she has given to community service projects and cocurricular activities.

The normal penalty for plagiarism for a senior is withholding the bachelor's degree for one year and a permanent notation on the student's transcript that he or she committed plagiarism.

Ingrid has been admitted to several top medical schools and, concerned about her future, has said publicly that she will sue the college for personal and material damages in the event of a guilty verdict.

Winnie also has received a memo from the college president saying, "Without wishing to influence the Student Judiciary Committee in any way, I am duty bound to tell you that this institution cannot afford the legal costs associated with lengthy litigation in this matter." Winnie knows that any judgment rendered by her committee could subsequently be reversed by the college administration.

What are Winnie's leadership responsibilities in this situation? How can she help her committee reach a decision that both satisfies the demands of fairness and protects the integrity and welfare of the college?

QUESTIONS TO GUIDE DISCUSSION

1. What is plagiarism exactly? Does what Ingrid did fit this definition? Is plagiarism sometimes accidental and unintentional? How often do you think it can be attributed to mere carelessness rather than intentional deceit? Is there reasonable doubt about Ingrid's guilt? Do you think the punishment at this college fits the crime?

2. How significant is the testimony of the character witness? Does it make any difference that this person is the Honors Program director? Is Ingrid's outstanding academic record relevant to the case?

3. What was Ingrid's motive for announcing her plans to sue in the event of a guilty verdict? If she is found guilty and goes through with her plan, how likely is it that the suit will be successful? Should this risk be taken into account, as the president suggests?

NOW WHAT IF?

- Ingrid is Winnie's roommate and best friend.
- The accused is a student with a spotty academic record and a history of conduct code violations.
- Amid copious tears, Ingrid candidly admits that she knowingly and willfully plagiarized, apologizes sincerely, agrees to rewrite the paper, and asks for clemency on the grounds of her past performance.

CASE IN POINT

Winnie and the college president must consider both the immediate and the long-term consequences of a guilty verdict in Ingrid's case. If the president overrules a guilty verdict for financial or political reasons, it could damage his or her credibility within the college community. As the college leader, the president also must be concerned with the long-term consequences of accepting and enforcing a guilty judgment. Such a course of action could have a disastrous effect on the college's future.

Leaders are often faced with what appear to be two incompatible or even contradictory paths to a decision. Review the following four sets of leadership principles and consider the paradoxes (apparent contradictions) they represent:

- Leaders must make rational decisions based on data and facts.

  Leaders need to consider emotional factors and make subjective judgments.

- Leaders need to resist opposition and maintain their positions under pressure.
  Leaders need to recognize when to change tactics and alter the game plan.

- Leaders need to respect protocol and provide structure for the group.
  Leaders need to know when to ignore the rules and adjust priorities.

- Leaders should endorse ethical principles and embody moral integrity.
  Leaders have obligations to others that sometimes require ethical compromise.

1. Can you think of other paradoxes that apply to leadership principles and/or decisions?
2. How do you explain this phenomenon of leadership principles that appear to be in conflict with each other? What do these sets of contradictory principles indicate about the nature of leadership?
3. Were any of the leadership paradoxes evident in your group discussion of this case?

WRITING ASSIGNMENT

In a personal journal entry (two handwritten pages), reflect on the topic of academic plagiarism—your own experiences with it and your feelings about it. Think back to your earliest school memories, when copying material from other sources was an accepted practice. Do you have a negative opinion of others who plagiarize, especially when grades are curved and your own grade may be lower than someone else's? Do you have questions about what constitutes plagiarism or about the penalties for those who get caught? Have you ever been tempted to plagiarize? Begin writing now—rapidly and freely.

SHOWTIME

<u>Cast of Characters</u>

STUDENT A Winnie
STUDENT B The instructor who has accused Ingrid of plagiarism
STUDENT C Ingrid
STUDENT D The Honors Program director, a character witness

<u>The Plot</u>

A hearing room.

Winnie begins by stating the case against Ingrid and the penalty in the event of a guilty verdict.

She then summons the instructor who accused Ingrid of plagiarism and asks the instructor to describe the alleged offense and any subsequent action.

After the instructor's testimony is complete, Winnie gives Ingrid an opportunity to respond. After stating her case, Winnie summons the Honors Program director as a character witness. The director praises Ingrid and asks the committee for leniency on her behalf.

Winnie then asks Ingrid if she has anything more to add. She does indeed. She describes her plans for medical school, the damages she is likely to suffer if found guilty, and her intention to file a lawsuit for personal and material damages in the event of a guilty verdict.

The committee goes into closed session. Winnie leads the discussion, with other class members portraying various committee members. They may adopt faculty roles of their own choosing.

In the course of their discussion, Winnie introduces the president's memo, noting its concern about the costs of litigation. The committee discusses the case further in light of the president's comments. Then they leave the room and take a vote. (The vote need not be unanimous. In this case, the majority rules.)

The committee returns to the room. Winnie announces both the verdict and the sentence and explains the committee's reasons for its actions.

The hearing is adjourned.

RESEARCH KIT

Print/On-line Resources

- Written composition style manuals—definitions of plagiarism
- Student conduct code
- College disciplinary procedures—academic dishonesty
- Gehring et al., *Issues and Perspectives on Academic Integrity* (NASPA Report, 1986)
- Maramark et al., *Academic Dishonesty Among College Students* (U.S. Department of Education, 1993)

Human Resources

- Dean of students
- College ombudsperson
- Department head
- Premedical student adviser
- Center for Academic Integrity, University of Maryland

The Midnight Hacker

Paul and his roommate, Jason, are best friends and share a passionate interest in computers. Paul's own interest has led him to create a small software company, which, after three years of hard work, is now yielding enough profits to pay his tuition.

Jason has gotten into the habit of sending software over the Internet to other computer enthusiasts; they in turn share software with him. Some of it is shareware (in the public domain), but much of it is copyrighted. This has been going on for some time. Paul has never criticized Jason for the practice, even though both know it's illegal. But now that Paul is developing software himself for commercial profit, he has acquired a new perspective.

When he expresses his concern, Jason defends his activities by saying that he would never pirate *Paul's* software, that he can't afford to buy expensive software, that the copyright law is unenforceable, and that the software companies are making millions and won't be significantly harmed by one person copying a program.

Paul values his friendship with Jason, but he also values respect for the law and realizes that failure to report criminal activity is itself a crime. What should he do?

QUESTIONS TO GUIDE DISCUSSION

1. Does Paul and Jason's friendship outweigh the legal considerations in this case?

2. What is the purpose of copyright law? If there were no copyright laws to worry about, would Paul still have a moral obligation not to profit from other people's work? If so, what is the basis of that obligation?

3. The law that requires witnesses to report a crime is a basic tenet of English common law, even though it is rarely prosecuted in the United States. Do you agree with this law? Under what circumstances would you choose to disregard it?

NOW WHAT IF?

▪ When Jason is out, Paul sneaks a peek at his computer and finds a copy of his own copyrighted software on Jason's hard drive.

▪ Paul has done a little software pirating himself, although he no longer does it. By turning Jason in, he runs the risk of being charged with the same crime.

▪ Paul is a composer-musician. Jason has been dubbing cassettes of new releases—including the original work of musicians who are Paul's friends.

CASE IN POINT

Technological advances in computers and information systems have changed the lives of students such as Jason and Paul. Electronic communications technology also has changed the relationship between leaders and followers. Electronic media (E-mail and the Internet, telecommunications, compressed video and satellite) allow leaders to exchange information and interact with large numbers of followers within the organization.

Examine the following list of issues raised by the revolution in electronic communications technology:

▪ Right to privacy

▪ Security of proprietary information (patents, personnel decisions)

▪ Information overload

▪ Impersonal atmosphere, reduction of human contact

▪ Elimination of nonverbal exchanges (eye contact, gestures, dress)

▪ Competitive advantage to people with advanced keyboard/computer expertise

1. In addition to the preceding list, what other issues of electronic communication (for leaders as well as followers) can you think of?

2. What are some positive aspects of the technological revolution (for leaders as well as followers)?

3. How has the traditional pattern of large organizations (top-down management, hierarchical reporting structures) been altered by electronic communications technology?

WRITING ASSIGNMENT

Most colleges today provide students with networked computer labs, shared access to servers and software, E-mail, and many more electronic aids to learning. What ethical issues and social problems have been created by this technological explosion? Describe an abuse of public computing resources that you find particularly annoying and propose a solution. Or write a case like those in this book involving a computing impropriety.[1]

SHOWTIME

In this role-playing exercise, Paul confronts Jason, expressing his concerns about his roommate's behavior in an effort to arrive at a mutually agreeable solution. The actors will do two improvisations, taking two different approaches.

First run-through.   Paul is confrontational, accusing Jason of wrongdoing and assigning blame. Jason defends himself in any way he can.

Second run-through.   Paul describes how he feels about what Jason is doing, while reassuring him that they will always be friends no matter what. He focuses on his own feelings rather than on Jason's actions. Jason listens carefully to what Paul is saying and responds as his respect and affection for Paul dictate.

After the second run-through, the audience should try to articulate what was different about the two versions and to identify the leadership behaviors exhibited by both men in the second run-through that helped to bring about an acceptable compromise.

---

[1] For more information on writing cases, see Selected Bibliography, "Teaching and Learning with Cases." For specific case examples, see especially M. Sumner, "Ethics Online," *Educom Review* (July-August 1996), 32–35.

RESEARCH KIT

Print/On-line Resources

- Federal copyright law
- Regulations of the Federal Communications Commission (FCC)—use of the Internet
- Local/state criminal conduct code
- Rules governing the use of campus computing facilities
- Articles on ethics in electronic communications

Human Resources

- College computing administrator
- College attorney
- Philosophy instructor who teaches ethics

A Crisis of Conscience

Tad couldn't believe his luck. The two documents lay side by side on his desk: his final grade report from Remington College, showing a cumulative grade point average (GPA) of 3.67, and his official transcript, showing a final GPA of 3.76. He had calculated and recalculated, and there was no doubt about it. Someone in the academic records office had made a data entry error and gotten him admitted to the University of Michigan Law School!

Tad was ambitious and knew that his political career would be jump-started by a degree from one of the nation's most prestigious law schools. Tad's Law School Admissions Test (LSAT) scores and recommendations were excellent, but his GPA fell below Michigan's required minimum of 3.75. Thanks to an errant keystroke made by a records clerk, he had made the cut!

His first instinct was to tell his roommates, Andy and Sven, about his acceptance and the error. Andy was pleased because he, too, had been admitted to Michigan, and now they could be roommates. Sven was less enthusiastic: he had gotten a 3.69 and had had to settle for a less presti-gious law school. That night Tad and Andy went out to celebrate, leaving Sven home alone to mull over his fate.

Tad awoke the next morning with a troubled conscience, his political ambitions at war with his principles. A leader in his young people's group at church and a mentor to troubled inner-city teens, Tad understood the difference between right and wrong. On the one hand, doing the right thing—notifying the Remington registrar and the Admissions Office at Michigan of the transcript error—would jeopardize his law school admis-sion and the distinguished law degree so important to a political career. On the other hand, ignoring the matter could haunt him later. If the mistake were uncovered—an unlikely possibility—his acceptance could be with-drawn and his political career jeopardized. Having told his roommates, he could never plead ignorance later. He knows Andy would never say anything, but he's not sure about Sven.

What should he do? What would *you* do?

QUESTIONS TO GUIDE DISCUSSION

1. Is Tad morally obligated to report the error? Are you aware of any legal requirements to do so?

2. Is there a statute of limitations on such clerical errors (a period of time after which the mistake can no longer be legally corrected)? Where would you go to find this out?

3. If Sven chooses to file a formal complaint, how should he proceed? Whom should he talk to first?

NOW WHAT IF?

■ Sven indicates that he plans to report the error to the proper authorities unless Tad can give him a good reason not to.

■ Tad discloses the error to his priest at confession and is told that he must first do everything in his power to correct the error before his contrition can be accepted as sincere.

■ Andy resents the fact that he worked hard to get into law school while Tad did not. He tells Tad that unless he reports the error, their friendship is over.

CASE IN POINT

Tad is an aspiring leader with professional ambitions. He hopes one day to be acknowledged as a leader, but will he measure up? And against what contemporary standards will he need to measure himself? What qualities are generally recognized today as signs of leadership potential, and why are some individuals singled out for leadership roles? Review the following list of qualities that could influence a person's selection or designation as a leader:

■ Respected or esteemed

■ Popular

■ Perceived to be friendly

■ Physically attractive

■ Intelligent

■ Influential

1. Are these all good reasons for selecting someone as a leader? Are there better reasons? As a group, create your own list. How is your list different from the preceding one?

2. Given Tad's situation, what qualities do you think are most important for him to consider or cultivate?

3. Are some of the qualities listed above more likely than others to result in a person's selection as a leader? Which ones are less consequential? What factors do you consider absolutely essential?

4. Do leadership qualities differ depending on the leadership context? What leadership qualities would you look for in each of the following positions?

   ▓ President of student government

   ▓ Captain of the football team

   ▓ Chief executive officer of a large corporation

   ▓ Fighter pilot squadron leader

   ▓ Chief scientist in a federal research laboratory

   To what extent do the qualities you listed for these positions overlap? Which ones are unique to the particular leadership context?

WRITING ASSIGNMENT

Pretend you are Tad and write a journal entry (two handwritten pages) framed as a debate between the two sides of Tad's nature—the person with a tender conscience and the person driven by self-interest and overweening ambition. Do not attempt to resolve the conflict, just show it.

SHOWTIME

The class is divided into two groups who stand facing each other: one group portrays the "good Tad," the other the "bad Tad."

Each person is given an opportunity to speak. The teams take turns speaking. A "bad Tad" volunteers to begin the debate. After a brief statement, the speaker sits down after tapping someone from his or her team on the shoulder. That person becomes the next speaker, and so on. Both sides state what they feel is the best course of action for Tad to take and refute the position taken by the other side. The last two people left standing must summarize their groups' positions.

RESEARCH KIT

Print/On-line Resources

- College policies and procedures—academic records
- Law school admissions policies and procedures
- College disciplinary procedure
- Civil law—fraud, misrepresentation, failure to disclose information known to be in error

Human Resources

- College registrar
- College and law school admissions officers
- College attorney
- Member of the clergy or college instructor who teaches ethics

A Buried Secret

While working at her day job at a waste management firm, Audrey became interested in geology and enrolled in an evening course in earth science at the local community college. While researching a paper on contaminated ground water, she came across some potentially explosive information. She learned that the college's new central administration building, recently completed with great fanfare, was situated on top of a large hazardous waste dump that had never been cleaned up.

Audrey expressed her concern to her earth science instructor, who informed the department head, who informed the dean, who informed the vice president, who informed the president. Now, months later, word has come back by the same route that the administration is unwilling to excavate on the strength of unsupported allegations by a student.

Audrey also suspects that local politicians were aware of the problem during the bidding and construction process but conspired in a cover-up to protect the donor of the land, a wealthy businessman who is now the U.S. representative from Audrey's district.

Audrey works forty hours a week and, as a single parent of two active pre-schoolers, is reluctant to become drawn into an issue that could drag on and on. At the same time, she is angry at the indifferent administrative response to her concern. If she is correct and the toxic materials pollute the ground water, the consequences could be disastrous for thousands of residents.

If she does pursue the matter, despite the obstacles she faces, what steps should she take and in what order?

QUESTIONS TO GUIDE DISCUSSION

1. What problems does the case present? In your group, list as many problems as you can on three-by-five-inch cards, one to a card. Then arrange the cards three different ways, according to the following criteria:

a. Most difficult to solve

b. Most important to me

c. Most important to others

Did your card arrangement differ significantly for each criterion? Which is the best criterion to use for identifying the core problem? Should all three be taken equally into account? What criteria would you add to the list?

2. Rank the following strategies in order of their likely effectiveness:

- Writing an E-mail message to the president of the college

- Writing a letter to the editor of the student newspaper

- Writing a letter to the editor of the local newspaper

- Collecting student signatures on a petition

- Contacting the state attorney general's office

- Contacting the Environmental Protection Agency (EPA) in Washington, D.C.

- Organizing a student boycott of classes

- Asking your student senator to raise the issue in government

- Forming a student committee on environmental safety

- Calling a meeting of all stakeholders

3. Does this case present a simple either-or choice between the public good and private welfare? Or is there a spectrum of choices between these two poles?

NOW WHAT IF?

- Audrey got her information from her boyfriend, the son of a member of the city council. He has asked her to keep her source confidential.

- Hazardous chemicals are a red flag to Audrey because her father, a veteran of the Vietnam War, died prematurely after being exposed to Agent Orange.

- Audrey's uncle, an attorney, is urging her to file a class-action suit against the college, but Audrey would have to prove in court that the college was negligent.

CASE IN POINT

Audrey's decision could be clarified by conducting a *personal leadership inventory*. Examine yourself as a potential leader in relation to the following probing questions:

- What are my motives for becoming a leader?
- What positive attributes or skills will enhance my ability to lead?
- What traits or behaviors limit my leadership potential?
- Whose leadership abilities do I admire and seek to emulate?
- In what specific situations have I exercised or failed to exercise leadership?

1. Summarize your answers to these questions and draw conclusions about your progress toward assuming a leadership role in your school or community.

2. What are your current areas of strength? In what areas do you need to improve?

3. How will a personal leadership inventory help Audrey in her encounters with the various constituencies in her community and college?

WRITING ASSIGNMENT

Write your own personal leadership inventory, addressing the questions listed in "Case in Point."

SHOWTIME

The class divides into three groups of equal size, each physically separate from the others and all facing the actor playing Audrey, who sits in front facing them. Group 1 represents *The Public Good;* Group 2 represents *Self-Interest;* Group 3 represents *Compromise*. Each group leaves one chair empty.

Members of the three groups use all their powers of persuasion to get Audrey to join them—that is, to declare her commitment to one of the three courses of action by sitting in that group's empty chair. Audrey is free to respond to any comment: she can agree, disagree, or remain silent.

The scene ends when she gets up and sits in one of the three empty chairs.

RESEARCH KIT

Print/On-line Resources

- Environmental organization home pages
- Studies of impact of hazardous waste on ground water
- Local building codes
- College bidding and construction policies—physical plant
- Federal, state, and local environmental legislation

Human Resources

- College health and safety officer
- Faculty member (geology/ecology—environmental specialist)
- Construction firm executive
- Consumer advocacy group leader
- Elected city/county official
- Physical plant administrator
- State/federal Occupational Safety and Health Administration (OSHA) official
- Environmental Protection Agency (EPA) official

The Charity Case

As treasurer of his fraternity, Dan is in a quandary. He believes the president of his fraternity, Max—who is also senior class president and a popular figure on campus—is stealing.

Recently, Dan's fraternity sponsored a rock concert to benefit a local homeless shelter. Hundreds of people attended the concert at five dollars a ticket. Max was to have deposited the gate receipts in the fraternity's account at a local bank (this secret account is against college rules—Greek organizations are required to use college accounts) and then written a check for one thousand dollars to the shelter.

Dan received a phone call from the shelter inquiring about the check, which they had not yet received. When Dan asked Max about it, he said that, after paying the band (which had demanded eight hundred dollars in cash), there was not enough money left for the shelter. The bank provided Dan with a copy of a check for eight hundred dollars dated the day after the concert—written by Max to himself. There were also several unexplained automatic teller machine (ATM) withdrawals in smaller amounts.

Max is away at a student leadership conference in Honolulu, a trip he is taking, according to a recent speech before the Student Senate, "at my own expense."

Dan has been too busy to monitor the fraternity's financial situation closely and needs all his free time to study for the Law School Admissions Test (LSAT). Should he look the other way? What is his responsibility to his fraternity?

QUESTIONS TO GUIDE DISCUSSION

1. What is the relation of Dan's role as fraternity treasurer to the roles of other leaders in the fraternity? How can he work with them on this problem so that the entire leadership team is strengthened?

2. What portions of your college's student conduct code are applicable to this case, if any? Is there sufficient evidence here to warrant criminal charges in a civil court? Can charges be brought in both civil court and a campus judicial hearing? Wouldn't this violate the Fifth Amendment protection of a defendant against double jeopardy (being tried twice on the same count)? Where would you go to get advice on these questions?

3. Once this particular situation is resolved, what procedures might be put in place to prevent this from happening in the future?

NOW WHAT IF?

- Rumor has it that at the Panhellenic Honors Banquet next week, Dan's fraternity will be awarded the Golden Palm for Service, the highest honor a campus organization can receive, for its efforts on behalf of the homeless.

- One of Dan's fraternity brothers suggests that he drop the whole thing because the evidence against Max is inconclusive and the college really doesn't need another fraternity scandal.

- The money had been deposited in a legitimate college account.

CASE IN POINT

It appears that Max has betrayed the trust invested in him by his fraternity brothers and failed his peers as a leader.

Review the following list of fundamental mistakes that ineffective leaders make, as outlined by J. K. Van Fleet in *The 22 Biggest Mistakes Managers Make*. Use the list to critique Max's behavior and to evaluate your own tendencies as a potential leader.

- Wastes time on tasks that should be delegated to others
- Refuses to take responsibility for his or her actions
- Tries to be popular rather than respected
- Exploits his or her position for personal gain
- Fails to ask subordinates for advice
- Defends authority rather than addresses the problem

1. Which of the mistakes noted above does Max appear to have made?
2. What other kinds of mistakes are sometimes made by young, inexperienced leaders?
3. Arrange your full list of leadership mistakes in order, from most serious to least serious.

WRITING ASSIGNMENT

Pretend you are Dan. Write a personal, confidential letter to Max letting him know that you have become aware of some potentially damaging information. Refrain from making accusations. Your challenge will be to allow Max to save face—either by explaining how what appears to be fraud is actually a misunderstanding or by confessing his misdeeds to you and trusting that you will help him set things straight. The language and tone of your letter will be crucial to evoking the right response.

SHOWTIME

This activity involves a game called hidden agenda.

Dan has notified the dean of students that there may be a problem involving Max and the homeless shelter. The dean has called a meeting to ascertain the facts and try to resolve the problem.

The actors playing Dan, Max, the dean of students, and the director of the homeless shelter sit in a circle. Each of them has a hidden agenda. These are written by the facilitator on three-by-five-inch sticky notes. Following are examples of a hidden agenda for each of the characters:

(Dan) wants Max expelled so he can be president

(Max) secretly in love with the dean of students

(Dean of students) under pressure to avoid a scandal

(Shelter director) in cahoots with Max—they divided the money

Before the action begins, the facilitator gives each actor a hidden agenda, which the actor reads and then places on his or her back so that the audience can see the agenda but the other actors cannot. The actors must try to guess each other's hidden agendas during the course of the meeting.

RESEARCH KIT

Print/On-line Resources

- Fraternity policies and procedures manuals
- College student handbook and code of conduct
- College business office procedures—student accounts
- College judicial process—nonacademic misconduct
- Civil and criminal codes—misdemeanor and felony theft

Human Resources

- Panhellenic Council official
- Dean of students
- Bank official
- College attorney
- College business affairs administrator

La Raza Derecha

La Raza Derecha is a small but influential organization of Hispanic students, faculty, staff, alumni, and local business leaders at a large south-western community college with a substantial Hispanic population. The group's unifying principle is political conservatism: they oppose special favors for minority groups, including race-based scholarships and affirmative action hiring practices. Some of its members are successful entrepreneurs or the sons and daughters of inherited wealth; they boast of having achieved the American dream through hard work, not through handouts.

Jorge, a student in the college's construction technology program, recently joined La Raza Derecha at the invitation of a friend. Even though he agrees with the group's conservative philosophy, he has managed to conceal from them the fact that he is himself the beneficiary of a full-tuition scholarship from the college's Hispanic Scholarship Fund, an endowment of more than $400,000. Jorge is a sixth-generation American from a middle-class family (his father is a drywall installer for a small construction firm), and although he was an indifferent student in high school, he was happy to accept the scholarship, which has enabled his father to purchase a new pickup truck.

La Raza Derecha has undertaken an active campaign to eliminate the Hispanic Scholarship Fund and all other race-based scholarships at the college. They argue that such scholarships are demeaning (minority scholarships require a 2.0 grade point average [GPA]—far below the 3.0 required for other scholarships), reward mediocrity rather than merit and healthy competition, and encourage self-defeating notions of victimization. They want Hispanic students to compete on a level playing field with all other Americans rather than hide behind their ethnic status.

Jorge has been asked to lead the student lobbying effort. On the one hand, if it is successful, he will be biting the hand that feeds him. On the other hand, these people are his friends, and he will need their support when he enters the business community in a few years. What should he do?

QUESTIONS TO GUIDE DISCUSSION

1. What values are in conflict in this case? What does Jorge value? La Raza Derecha? The college? What common ground, if any, do these parties all share?

2. In the mid-1990s, some federal district court judges ruled that scholarships that discriminate on the basis of race are a violation of civil rights. Would this judgment have been different if the scholarships had come from an endowed source (private gifts) rather than from public tax dollars? Even if the practice is legal, what do you think of it on moral grounds?

3. Is it legally possible to eliminate an endowment or to convert it to some other use? If the purpose of the endowment was fairly general—say, to improve conditions for the Hispanic community—what are some alternative uses for it?

NOW WHAT IF?

▨   Jorge is about to graduate and has been offered a job by a member of La Raza Derecha.

▨   Jorge has affluent parents who could easily afford to finance his education.

▨   Other minority groups on campus have asked for Jorge's support in the lobbying effort.

CASE IN POINT

In his 1988 text *Taking Charge,* P. M. Smith lists twenty fundamentals that should characterize a leader. Examine the following excerpted selection of Smith's leadership fundamentals in relation to Jorge's dilemma:

▨   Trust is vital.

▨   Leaders must provide vision.

▨   Leaders must subordinate their ambition and egos to the goals of the unit or institution they lead.

▨   Leaders must be motivators.

▨   Leaders should be reliable.

▨   Leaders should exude integrity.

1. What additional leadership fundamentals relate particularly to Jorge's leadership challenge?
2. Which of the fundamentals noted above or in your expanded list are most critical to Jorge's success as a potential leader with La Raza Derecha? Why?
3. Do you possess the leadership fundamentals listed above? In which areas do you need additional work or experience?

WRITING ASSIGNMENT

Jorge has decided to withdraw from La Raza Derecha because he has examined his conscience and finds that he disagrees with the organization's fundamental principles. Compose his letter of resignation.

OR

Jorge has come to the conclusion that he will support the campaign to eliminate preferential treatment for minorities at the university even if it means a personal financial loss. Compose the text for a flier that Jorge will distribute on campus urging Hispanic students, faculty, and staff to join the campaign.

SHOWTIME

Students pair up and interview each other on the subject of awarding scholarships restricted to members of recognized minorities or underrepresented groups. Ask the following questions, then make up two additional questions of your own:

1. Do you think scholarships should be awarded on the basis of such characteristics as race, ethnicity, or gender? Why or why not?
2. Does it make any difference if the scholarship is funded by taxes or by private donors, or if the college is public or private?
3. _____

    _____
4. _____

    _____

Take no more than five minutes for each interview (ten minutes total). Then share what you learned with the entire class.

RESEARCH KIT

Print/On-line Resources

- Admissions/scholarship criteria
- Articles for or against affirmative action or race-based scholarships
- State/federal affirmative action legislation
- Studies of impact of financial aid on college success

Human Resources

- Financial aid officer
- Minority program administrator
- Prominent minority alumni
- Minority faculty member (for or against affirmative action)
- State/federal legislator or judge
- Student affairs administrator

Leadership and Individual Rights

A major challenge for student leaders is finding a proper balance between freedom and responsibility, between their own self-interest and their commitment to the welfare of the larger community. The cases in Part Two focus on this dilemma: what happens when individual rights and social responsibility appear to be in conflict?

The Defender's Dilemma

Certain administrators have been cracking down on student expression. First, the editor of the student newspaper was fired for an editorial (weak on evidence, but an entertaining piece) that referred to the college president as a "limp-wristed neo-Nazi." Then Spike Lee's guest appearance was canceled when it was allegedly rumored that he was planning to encourage black athletes to boycott the football and basketball teams.

By way of response, Sandy and several other prelaw students have formed a new student organization, Student Activists for Free Expression (SAFE). The group's constitution, much publicized around campus in brochures and posters, pledges to defend the First Amendment rights of all students, regardless of their views.

A student named Gordon approaches Sandy asking that SAFE defend him during his appearance before the Judicial Board. Gordon has been kicked out of his sociology class (a decision upheld by the dean) because of the T-shirts he insists on wearing, which feature such slogans as FREE JAMES EARL RAY, THE BELL CURVE WAS RIGHT, and HITLER HAD A GOOD IDEA.

Many of the members of Sandy's fledgling organization are African American and Jewish students, who are outraged that the group would even consider defending such blatant racism. How should Sandy respond to Gordon's request and to the outrage of the other members?

QUESTIONS TO GUIDE DISCUSSION

1. What issues—legal, political, and moral—are involved in this case? Are they all equally important? What do you do when moral law and civil law appear to be in conflict? What do you do when it is not politically expedient to do the right thing? Is it sometimes necessary to commit a small wrong so that a greater good will result? Can you think of examples in history? In your own experience?

31

2. The American Civil Liberties Union (ACLU), a privately supported organization, often faces dilemmas of this sort. How does it handle them?

3. Was the editor guilty of slander in calling the college president a "limp-wristed neo-Nazi?"

NOW WHAT IF?

▪ Gordon is African American. His T-shirts read: A JEW MADE ME A SLAVE and JEWS KILLED JESUS. Some of SAFE's members are African American students who agree with these sentiments.

▪ The wealthy father of one of SAFE's Jewish members has offered to deposit $10,000 in the group's legal defense fund if it agrees not to accept Gordon's case. Sandy knows that SAFE could defend a lot more students with $10,000 than with its current budget balance of $39.08.

▪ A conservative national radio call-in show host picks up on the case, publicly accusing SAFE of self-contradiction and hypocrisy. Sandy is challenged by the host to call the show and defend SAFE's views.

CASE IN POINT

Sandy and the other members of SAFE have a number of managerial and leadership tasks to perform. These include the following:

▪ Establishing SAFE as a legitimate campus organization (this requires a constitution and bylaws approved by the dean of students)

▪ Creating vision and mission statements

▪ Creating a strategic plan and mobilizing the organization for action

▪ Ensuring effective communication within the group and between the group and its external stakeholders

There are immediate decisions to be made as well.

Recent leadership research distinguishes the role of manager from the role of leader. In *On Leadership*, John Gardner argues that such a distinction is artificial and misleading. He proposes the concept of a *leader/manager* who is distinguished by the following traits:

▪ Thinks long term, beyond the immediate crisis

▪ Considers conditions external to the organization and broadens the problem-solving context

▪ Influences and interacts with organizations beyond the group's boundaries and seeks cooperative alliances

- Stresses the intangibles of vision, values, and motivation
- Coordinates multiple, possibly conflicting, subgroups
- Seeks to renew, revise, and restructure even while supporting the existing organizational process

1. Are there meaningful distinctions to be made between the terms *leader* and *manager,* or do you agree with Gardner? Explain.
2. What aspects of the leader/manager model can Sandy use to lead and manage SAFE?
3. Are there arenas of leadership in which you see leader/managers operating? Cite specific examples.

WRITING ASSIGNMENT

Pretend you are a committed member of SAFE. You have been asked by the leader of the group to compose the SAFE Bill of Student Rights, which will affirm the right of all students to self-expression, however unpopular, controversial, or repugnant that expression may be. SAFE's intention is to forward your document to the Student Senate, as the basis for a free speech code for all students on campus.

SHOWTIME

Cast of Characters

STUDENT A Sandy, the founder of SAFE
STUDENT B The fired editor of the student paper, now a member of SAFE
STUDENT C A Jewish member of SAFE
STUDENT D An African American member of SAFE
STUDENT E Gordon

The Plot

A living room in an off-campus apartment.

Members of SAFE are conducting business when the doorbell rings. Gordon enters, explains his dilemma, asks SAFE to represent him at his hearing before the Judicial Board, and then leaves.

Members proceed to discuss the merits of the case—on legal, moral, and political grounds.

A Jewish member leaves to make a phone call and returns with news of her father's ten-thousand-dollar offer.

The discussion continues and ends when Sandy says, "Well, I'm glad we were able to reach an agreement."

RESEARCH KIT

Print/On-line Resources

- U.S. Constitution (Bill of Rights, First Amendment)
- College student handbook and code of conduct
- Campus speech codes
- Federal (Department of Education) regulations (hostile environment)
- Federal case law precedent (*Doe* v. *University of Michigan,* 1989)

Human Resources

- Student government leaders
- ACLU representative
- Editor of campus newspaper
- College or private attorney
- Law professor
- College student affairs administrator

Armed and Dangerous

When Hakeem left his family, friends, and native Nigeria to live in America and study at the state university, he took with him a number of prized possessions that had been given to him for safekeeping by the spiritual leader of his clan. Among them was a sacred spear decorated with egret and parrot feathers that had belonged to his grandfather and various ceremonial bows and arrows regarded as religious objects to be used in spiritual rituals.

Not long into the fall semester, two alarming incidents raised the issue of campus safety: a female student was raped at knifepoint in the bushes outside her residence hall, and a male student was threatened with a handgun in an early-morning melee in the student union parking lot.

University administrators responded with alacrity. The police chief issued a policy statement saying that "any firearm or weapon in possession of students on land controlled by the Board of Regents will be confiscated." The dean of students, citing an obscure clause in the university housing contract ("possession of firearms, dangerous weapons, hunting arrows, or potentially injurious war souvenirs is grounds for eviction"), ordered a room search, in the course of which Hakeem's sacred artifacts were confiscated.

Hakeem was outraged and lodged an immediate complaint with the director of housing. "These are not weapons," he argued. "These are like what Bibles or menorahs are to Christians and Jews. Seizing them is tantamount to religious persecution!" The housing director responded that if Hakeem were allowed to keep his weapons, other students would make similar demands to keep knives and handguns.

Hakeem then wrote a letter to the student newspaper, explaining that the artifacts were sources of spiritual confirmation for him. Another student wrote a letter in a subsequent issue, noting sarcastically that he felt "spiritually confirmed by having a loaded .22 in my dresser drawer." Another letter writer claimed that the seizure was discriminatory, noting that Reserve Officers' Training Corps (ROTC) students are allowed to keep their weapons.

Now the issue has been picked up by the national media, and the dean of students has convened a task force to review the current policy. Barry, who is Hakeem's resident adviser, has been asked to serve on the task force as a student representative and to offer a constructive solution to the crisis at an upcoming meeting. How should Barry, who is responsible for the safety of some two hundred hall residents, prepare for the meeting?

QUESTIONS TO GUIDE DISCUSSION

1.   What individual rights are in conflict here? Are there more than two? Does one right have priority over another? If so, under what circumstances? If not, how are such conflicts best resolved?

2.   Is this a case in which the authorities should enforce the spirit rather than the letter of the law? Should Barry urge the task force to grant an exception to Hakeem? To ROTC? What are the possible negative consequences of granting exceptions to established institutional policies and procedures?

3.   Is the university responsible for the safety of its students, even if students behave illegally or irresponsibly? To what extent is an institution responsible (liable for damages) in the following cases?

   a.   Students are dancing and drinking on the roof of their residence hall; one of them slips and falls over the edge, paralyzing both legs.

   b.   A student is raped in the bushes in an unlighted area of campus.

   c.   A student is placed in the trunk of a car during a fraternity hazing, is abandoned, and suffocates.

   d.   A drunken student ignores warning signs at a construction site, climbs over a barbed wire fence, breaks into a laboratory, and is exposed to radiation.

NOW WHAT IF?

▪   Hakeem is assured that his weapons will be safely stored and returned to him when he leaves the university.

▪   Barry is a member of the National Rifle Association (NRA) and strongly believes in the constitutional right of all Americans to bear arms.

▪   Student government leaders and the campus newspaper editors come out in support of Hakeem's position and threaten to stage a demonstration that could embarrass the university's administration.

CASE IN POINT

The customs, language, and rituals of leaders often vary from culture to culture. American business leaders who want to conduct business in Japan, for example, have to adopt the values of Japanese business: patience, elaborate courtesy, and indirection. The following exercise highlights both the differences and the similarities of leadership roles as expressed in different cultural and historical contexts. In his biography of the Sioux chief Sitting Bull, *The Lance and the Shield*, Robert Utley summarizes the qualities of leadership as measured by the Sioux nation.

- *Bravery.* Highly regarded as a mark of leadership; individual valor more valued than group achievements; the most complete expression of bravery is to risk one's life without fear.
- *Fortitude.* Another manifestation of virtuous leadership; fortitude involves the ability to withstand pain without showing distress; an uncomplaining stoicism.
- *Generosity.* A leader's virtue is measured by how much, to whom, and in what manner he gives gifts and shares wealth; the leader disdains accumulating personal property and material goods.
- *Wisdom.* A reflection of a leader's excellence in the other three areas; represents the perspective and wisdom gained through an active spiritual life; the rarest of the four qualities.

1. What is unique about the leadership values of the Sioux?
2. What do the Sioux leadership values reveal about their cultural values?
3. What leadership expressions do the Sioux prize that are in conflict with those of the white culture that opposed and conquered them? What leadership values do the two antagonist groups share?
4. What leadership qualities revered by the Sioux are still highly valued in contemporary American society?
5. Can you draw any conclusions about universally accepted leadership values?

WRITING ASSIGNMENT

Conduct an opinion survey among a diverse group of students. Describe the case and ask them how they think it should be resolved. Classify and summarize the responses. Was there general agreement in favor of or against the weapons policy? If responses were divided, were they divided along racial, ethnic, age, or gender lines? Did the issue generate strong feelings or apathy? Do you think your survey accurately reveals the likely breakdown of opinion among the student body in general?

SHOWTIME

The task force has agreed that the policy is necessary to ensure the safety of students but is willing to consider allowing certain exceptions: weapons that are religious artifacts, weapons necessary for military science instruction, and any others the class wants to suggest.

The discussion takes place in a "fishbowl" format—seven chairs in the center of the room with the rest of the class seated around the perimeter. The facilitator serves as chair; he or she may ask for clarification and guide the discussion but does not make substantive comments. Five students participate in the task force; the chair to the facilitator's left is vacant.

Students outside the fishbowl may join the discussion at any time by sitting in the empty seat. When this happens, the student sitting on that person's left leaves the fishbowl, creating a new empty seat. The process continues clockwise until the agenda is completed (thirty to forty-five minutes).

RESEARCH KIT ▨▨▨▨▨▨▨▨▨▨▨▨

Print/On-line Resources

- Bill of Rights (freedom of religion, right to bear arms, unlawful search and seizure)
- College student handbook and code of conduct
- Residence hall contract
- College insurance/liability policies
- Civil law (weapons possession)

Human Resources

- Housing official
- Campus police/public safety officer
- Dean of students
- Member of the clergy
- College attorney
- NRA spokesperson

What's Wrong with This Picture?

One of the films routinely projected in a cinema course at a public university in the Midwest is *Taxi zum Klo*, a widely praised film whose protagonist is a gay schoolteacher. After a student objected to the film's homosexual content in a letter to the local newspaper, the following sequence of events occurred:

1. Acting independently, a grandstanding university board member held a press conference, deploring the university's use of taxpayers' money "to promote public degeneracy." This story made headlines in the local newspaper and was picked up by a wire service for national distribution.

2. The university president communicated the board member's concerns to the Student Senate (an elected representative body) and urged it to adopt a student rights policy requiring faculty to "warn students in advance about any sexual materials that might be used in class." The policy was approved, subject to Faculty Senate approval.

3. The Faculty Senate, an elective group that advises the vice president for academic affairs on policy matters, agreed to the policy, provided the word *sexual* was deleted.

4. This revision was rejected by the vice president for academic affairs, who, under pressure from the president, added the phrase "and to give students adequate warning of any unusual or unexpected class presentations or material."

5. The president placed the policy on the board's agenda, to be voted on at its next meeting.

6. Meanwhile, a group of students and faculty calling itself the Academic Freedom Coalition (AFC) began protesting what they perceived to be an assault on academic freedom. The AFC set up a literature table in the quad and rallied supporters with a bullhorn.

7. The campus police arrived and asked the leaders of the protest to identify themselves. When they refused, the police took photographs of the protesters. A photographer from the campus paper arrived and began to photograph the police taking photographs.

8. A scuffle ensued and developed into an all-night, full-scale riot. Local police were brought in, and tear gas and dogs were used to dispel the crowd. Several students and a faculty member were arrested.

9. A small group of students seized the administration building, refusing to leave until the president agreed to the nonnegotiable demands in the Manifesto of Academic Freedom they had composed.

10. The board's chairperson told the president that if she yielded to the students' demands, it would be her last official act as president.

What went wrong here? What might have been done differently at each stage to bring about a more positive outcome?

QUESTIONS TO GUIDE DISCUSSION

1. To whom are each of the following accountable: the film instructor, the board member, the president, the student senators, the faculty senators, and the vice president for academic affairs? Did they all behave accountably? Did they all behave responsibly? What is the difference, if any, between accountability and responsibility?

2. What leadership errors occurred in the case? What would have constituted responsible and effective leadership behavior by the principals in the case?

3. The current legal basis for banning books and films as pornographic or obscene is "community standards" (courts recognize that tastes and standards vary widely from one community to the next). Does this basis apply to the college classroom? In other words, does it matter if a majority of students in a class find certain material objectionable?

NOW WHAT IF?

▪ The offending film had not been an underground classic widely praised by knowledgeable critics but an ordinary "adult film" with little if any redeeming social value.

▪ A wealthy alumnus refused to honor his pledge to finance the new hockey rink unless a censorship policy was approved and enforced.

▪ The incident had occurred at a private rather than a public institution.

CASE IN POINT

Institutions of higher education have traditionally operated under a system of *shared governance* in which the lines of authority are shifting and often ambiguous. Frequent and clear communication in this kind of setting—among and between board members, administrators, faculty, and students—is both extremely important and extremely difficult.

Effective leaders must be successful communicators. Examine the following list of behaviors or characteristics that describe the communication of an effective leader in a group setting:

- Attentive listener
- Friendly, accepting demeanor
- Charismatic, engaging
- Perceived honesty and integrity
- Asks questions
- Receptive to new initiatives

1. What other behaviors would enhance a leader's communication with his or her followers?
2. Which of the behaviors noted above were missing in the groups' interactions in this case?
3. Which of the behaviors are most critical to productive communication between leaders and followers?
4. What are your strengths as a communicator? In what areas do you need to improve?

WRITING ASSIGNMENT

Rewrite the story by changing at least one of the events so that a more positive outcome results. You may change the story at any point you wish, but try to find the point of no return—the critical moment when a positive outcome is still possible if wisdom, decency, and common sense prevail.

SHOWTIME

First, identify all the two-party conflicts in this case and write them on the board: student v. instructor, vice president for academic affairs v. faculty, AFC v. campus police, and so on.

Select the three conflicts you believe are most central to the case.

Place two chairs in front of each of the three conflicts listed on the board. Six students volunteer to represent each of the six parties in conflict. Each of the three conflicts will be mediated by the class as follows.

Speakers take turns briefly (1) describing the conflict from their point of view, (2) expressing how they feel about the other party's behavior, and (3) stating what they would consider to be an adequate remedy. Audience members may interrupt at any point but only to ask for further clarification.

At the conclusion of each of the three presentations, audience members may propose a solution or agreement, which may or may not be accepted by both parties. If a solution is unacceptable to one or both parties, negotiation continues until both agree.

(Note: Each session should take about fifteen minutes. If time is short, select one or two conflicts for negotiation.)

RESEARCH KIT

Print/On-line Resources

- Bill of Rights (freedom of expression)
- Faculty and student handbooks
- College policy/procedures manuals
- Articles on protest as free speech
- Statements on "Academic Freedom" and "Shared Governance" from American Association of University Professors (AAUP) "red book"
- Federal case law precedent (*Bethel School District #403* v. *Fraser,* 1986)

Human Resources

- Faculty government or faculty union leaders
- Cinema studies professor
- Board member
- Vice president for academic affairs
- Campus police chief
- Law professor or college attorney

The Mind of the Beholder

Eve, an older student majoring in art history at Firestone College, a church-related institution in the Deep South, is president of the Student Art Association, which is responsible for mounting the annual Student Art Exhibit in the narthex of the campus chapel. The association is responsible for selecting the exhibited works, which are automatically entered into competition for the lucrative Harry M. Baker Prize for Best of Show. Baker, who contributed the endowment for the prize, is a wealthy Firestone alumnus who, though elderly, continues to take an active interest in the competition. Winners are selected by a panel of judges, usually the Art Department faculty.

This year's winner has generated heated controversy. Mystifyingly titled *Mr. Magoo,* the work consists of various items pinned to a clothesline. Among them are a brassiere, a jockstrap, a rosary, a condom, a pocket New Testament, and other items of a sexual or religious nature. The viewer is supposed to look at the work through a pair of novelty-store eyeglasses mounted on a prie-dieu.

Baker, shocked and horrified by this assault on the spiritual values espoused by Firestone College, has threatened to withdraw his financial support unless the judges reconsider their decision and award the prize to another work that he prefers—a poorly executed pastel portraying Jesus' miracle at Cana.

Firestone's dean has gone a step further, canceling the show and ordering the destruction of six thousand copies of the alumni magazine, which contained a photo of the award-winning work and was about to be mailed. The dean also has ruled that in the future all literary and artistic works for public exhibition will be screened for content that might be offensive.

Eve and her friends in the Student Art Association are outraged at this suppression of artistic freedom and blatant censorship. Although many of the humanities faculty support the students, most faculty, staff, and students either believe that the dean did the right thing or are indifferent to the controversy.

What are the students' rights and responsibilities at this stage? If they choose to protest the decision, what is their best course of action? What outcomes can they hope to achieve? What should Eve's role be in the process?

QUESTIONS TO GUIDE DISCUSSION

1. Does it make any difference that this is a private rather than a public college? Do First Amendment rights enjoy the same protection in a private setting as at a state-supported college or university?
2. Are the intentions of the artist relevant here? If the meaning of the work was misunderstood, does that mean the artist failed and should not have won the prize in the first place?
3. Are there occasions when the wishes of a major donor ought to outweigh a student's freedom of expression?

NOW WHAT IF?

▨ *Mr. Magoo* was proclaimed a "satiric masterpiece" by a famous art critic and subsequently purchased for six figures by a major collector.

▨ The artist was known to be a deeply religious person or a sacrilegious rebel.

▨ Baker didn't particularly like *Mr. Magoo* as a work of art, but after the dean censors the work, he reverses his position and publicly supports Eve and the Student Art Association in their opposition to the censorship.

CASE IN POINT

Leaders cannot lead unless there are followers. Effective leaders respond to the motives and needs of those who fill supporting roles.

As president of the Student Art Association and as a more experienced older student on a campus where most students are of traditional college age, Eve is in a position to influence campus opinion in significant ways. She will need followers who support her leadership status and endorse her initiatives.

What do followers look for in a leader? Consider the following:

▨ Shows concern for followers as individuals
▨ Sets clear expectations for group and individual performance
▨ Recognizes and praises followers for work well done
▨ Makes followers feel relaxed
▨ Provides clear direction and structure for the contributions of followers.

1. Identify other positive attitudes toward followers that you look for in a leader.

2. Which of the behaviors could Eve use in this crisis? How?

3. What makes a good follower? Construct a list of positive "followership" traits. In what ways do you embody these traits? Have you ever resisted someone else's leadership? Does this mean you were a bad follower? Explain.

4. In which areas or ways do leaders sometimes disappoint or fail their followers?

WRITING ASSIGNMENT

Imagine you are writing a history of Firestone College and the events described above happened many years ago. You have just described the actual events. Now, in a page or two, describe the meaning of these events in Firestone's history. What lessons were learned by the board of trustees, the protesting students, and the college community?

SHOWTIME

Cast of Characters

STUDENT A The Dean
STUDENT B Eve
STUDENT C Mr. Baker
STUDENT D A local minister
STUDENT E A professor at Firestone
STUDENT F A member of the Alumni Association
STUDENT G The football coach
STUDENT H The artist who created Mr. Magoo

The Plot

In an effort to resolve the controversy, the dean has assembled a focus group consisting of various members of the college community. They have just finished lunch and have gotten to know each other a bit.

The dean sits at the head of a banquet table and officiates. He or she suggests that the members go around the table and introduce themselves, briefly stating the nature of their involvement in the current controversy and their views of it.

The discussion continues, with the dean functioning largely as facilitator and referee, and ends when the dean looks up at the clock and discovers that he or she is late for a meeting with the Board of Trustees.

RESEARCH KIT

Print/On-line Resources

- Bill of Rights (freedom of expression)
- Student handbook
- Policies on approval of student organizations
- College policies/procedures manuals
- Articles on censorship of works of art
- Federal case law precedent (*Joyner* v. *Whiting*, 1973)

Human Resources

- Student or faculty member (art or literature)
- Director of alumni or development office
- Art critic/reviewer
- Law professor or college attorney
- Dean (humanities)
- Major donor

The Loneliness of the Long-Distance Runner

Doug had been a star member of his high school track team, specializing in distance events. Because his school was small, he was not offered an athletic scholarship. He chose to enroll at Central State because its track team accepted walk-ons.

Recent changes in National Collegiate Athletic Association (NCAA) and conference rules intended to create gender equity for athletes have prompted Central State to make some changes in its athletic program. The rules changes require that the school add two new women's sports—soccer and golf—and that it achieve greater parity in the number of men and women involved in intercollegiate athletics.

At a special meeting, the head coach of the men's track team has announced that the size of the team will be reduced from 120 to 70. Doug is one of the 50 athletes who will be cut from the team for the upcoming season.

Doug has made great progress in his 10,000-meter event and believes that, with an additional year of training, he could qualify for an athletic scholarship to another school. He now feels that he is being discriminated against because he is male. He is thinking of filing suit against the university on the grounds of gender discrimination. Does Doug have a case?

QUESTIONS TO GUIDE DISCUSSION

1. Do you think correcting a historical pattern of unfairness to one group is justified even if it results in unfairness to another group? What do you think is the best way to correct a historical imbalance of this type?

2. Should the revenue-generating college sports—mainly football and basketball—be treated differently from other sports? Should the level of

student interest by gender in a given sport be a consideration in gender-equity decisions?

3. How is the issue of gender equity related to issues of race-based scholarships (see "La Raza Derecha," page 25)? To affirmative action? How are these issues different?

NOW WHAT IF?

■   Doug is a good athlete but will never be good enough to qualify for a scholarship.

■   Doug is a minority student.

■   Doug already has an academic scholarship and, according to federal guidelines, has no demonstrable financial need.

CASE IN POINT

If Doug pursues a suit against the university, it would change his life: he could well place himself at the center of a prolonged, perhaps national, controversy. Or he could simply drop the issue and accept his fate.

In *On Leadership*, John Gardner laments that many of the brightest and best young leaders of the 1960s were, for whatever reason, disinclined to seek out leadership opportunities and responsibilities. He found the young people of his era to be apathetic, cynical, and unresponsive to the challenges of leadership that presented themselves.

Reflect on Gardner's thesis. Does it accurately describe the situation in 1965 (the early days of the civil rights movement and the student protest against the war in Vietnam)? Does it accurately describe today's generation of college students?

1. Is it possible to generalize about an entire generation's attitudes toward leadership? Do societies maintain a consistent idea of leadership? What historical events have altered your own perception of leadership principles?

2. What social and political conditions may have influenced Gardner's viewpoint on leadership in the 1960s? To what extent have these factors remained the same or changed over the last thirty years?

3. Do you think the attitudes of young people toward leadership values and responsibilities will be dramatically different thirty years from now? If so, in what ways?

WRITING ASSIGNMENT

Define the concept of gender equity. How does the NCAA define it? How do you define it? Does it mean the same thing as *gender equality*? If not, what is the difference? What are some of the legal, educational, sexual, political, economic, and ideological dimensions of the latter term?

SHOWTIME

Divide the class into two groups, Pro and Con (anyone may sit on either side) and debate the following issue:

> **Resolved:** That all scholarships based on athletic or academic ability be abolished and that financial aid be distributed only on the basis of need.

Students who change their minds during the course of the debate should move their chairs to the other side.

The debate should have a stated time limit. When the time is up, the side with the most students is declared the winner.

RESEARCH KIT

Print/On-line Resources

- NCAA conference and college policies on gender equity
- Federal law (affirmative action, civil rights, gender equity) and case law precedent (*Kelley* v. *Board of Trustees of the University of Illinois,* 1993)
- Athletic scholarship guidelines
- Articles on gender discrimination/equity

Human Resources

- Athletic director
- Faculty representative to NCAA
- Male and female athletic (track) coaches
- Private attorney specializing in gender discrimination cases

The Coach Who Talked Trash

The men's basketball coach at Mountjoy College is an intense, street-smart man who cares as deeply about his players as he does about winning. He has challenged all his players to go beyond their limits, both on the basketball court and in the classroom. Although he is white, he grew up in the inner-city projects and has espoused an up-tempo, trash-talking, run-and-gun style of play that has brought the team national attention.

Recently during a halftime talk, trying to rouse his players after a sluggish first half, he said, "We need more niggers on this team." Most of the players understood what he meant—that the team needed to play more aggressively—but some players took offense and reported the coach's remarks the next day to the campus Judicial Board. Within twenty-four hours, the president of the college had suspended the coach without pay pending the results of a board investigation.

Recent events at Mountjoy have complicated the board's deliberations. In the wake of several serious racial incidents, the college recently adopted a strict speech code that forbids, among other things, race-based verbal harassment.

The Judicial Board consists of four faculty, four administrators, and one student, Pat, who has voting rights and often casts the swing vote that decides a close case. The board must recommend one of three courses of action: reinstatement with a reprimand and loss of pay; immediate termination of the coach's contract; or reinstatement with full back pay.

The board has now heard all the testimony and must vote on the coach's fate. What factors should Pat take into account in deciding how to vote? Which of these factors, if any, should be considered overriding and decisive?

QUESTIONS TO GUIDE DISCUSSION

1. Were the coach's remarks intended as a racial slur? Were they interpreted as such by the players? Are the coach's intentions or the players' interpretations relevant? Explain your answers.

2. Does the coach have a responsibility not only for what he says but for other people's perceptions of what he says? Explain.

3. How are each of the three possible outcomes likely to be interpreted by the college community? By students of color? By the news media?

NOW WHAT IF?

▓ The coach was African American.

▓ The coach had said, "You guys are playing like women."

▓ The incident was picked up by a wire service and quickly became a front-page story.

CASE IN POINT

As a representative of the students, Pat feels a strong obligation to be an active member of the Judicial Board. At the same time, Pat does not bring much authority to the board and has only limited power to influence its decisions. Nevertheless, Pat has the potential and the opportunity to emerge as a leader on behalf of the student body.

In *Leadership: A Communication Perspective,* Michael Hackman and Craig Johnson isolate the positive behaviors that are essential to leadership emergence.

▓ Participate early and often.

▓ Focus on communication quality as well as quantity.

▓ Demonstrate your competence to help the group complete the task.

▓ Help build the team into a cohesive unit.

1. What other behaviors, attitudes, or communication efforts will contribute to the emergence of a leader in a group?

2. How can Pat specifically use the four approaches noted above to function effectively as a leader in the group?

3. Which of the above behaviors characterize your efforts to emerge or express yourself as a leader? In which areas have you been reluctant or deficient?

WRITING ASSIGNMENT

The Judicial Board has been given three options in ruling on the coach's fate. State the option you recommend and provide a detailed rationale for your verdict. Before making your decision, consult whatever policies may have been adopted on your campus concerning discriminatory harassment, and be sure your decision is consistent with those policies. You are not obligated to reflect the consensus expressed by your group; you should support your personal view of what constitutes justice in this case.

SHOWTIME

Three students volunteer to address the class, each speaking for no more than five minutes in support of one of the three possible rulings in the case. Then the audience votes by secret ballot on the three rulings. After the results have been announced, discuss the effectiveness of the arguments for each of the three positions.

RESEARCH KIT

Print/On-line Resources

- Bill of Rights (free speech)
- College speech codes (hateful/inflammatory speech, hostile environment)
- Dismissal policies/procedures for athletic coaches
- College judicial appeal process
- Federal case law precedent (*Frisby* v. *Schultz,* 1988)

Human Resources

- Basketball coach
- Athletic director
- Faculty representative to National Collegiate Athletic Association (NCAA) or college athletic council
- African American studies faculty member or program director
- College or private attorney

Leadership and Diversity

Today's college campus, like the United States it-self, is a tossed salad of cultures. Wise campus leaders take advantage of this diversity by seeking out different points of view that help them make better decisions. Those who appreciate diversity are preparing themselves well for a future in which all cultures and nations will depend on each other for survival. America's labor force, which is daily becoming more culturally diverse, needs leaders who value the uniqueness and differences of the people they serve.

Logomania

It began with a subdued memo from the state's Bureau of Indian Affairs urging public schools and colleges with team names, mascots, and logos that could be considered demeaning to Native Americans to convert to other symbols.

The athletic teams at Fairfax State had been the Choctaws since time immemorial. Their logo was a profile of a brave in war paint. The football team mascot was Cheroot, a cigar-store Indian who entertained the crowd with loony antics. Fans were accustomed to an electrifying pregame ritual in which a shrieking "warrior" (usually a white student who had won the honor) raced across the field and planted a flaming spear on the fifty-yard line.

The new president at Fairfax, eager to please a state legislature dominated by Democrats, responded readily to the bureau's request by forming a committee consisting of a board member, two faculty members, two administrators, an alumnus, and one Native American student. They decided that the Choctaw must go and held a contest to choose a new name. The president announced the winner: "Henceforth, we are the Fairfax State Eagles!"

Now the campus is in an uproar. Booster organizations (called Warrior Clubs) and alumni groups are outraged. They have accused the president of caving in to political correctness at the expense of cherished traditions. Many are threatening to withhold their gifts until the action is rescinded. The Athletic Department is in despair, since the sale of licensed Choctaw items enriches their purse by more than a million dollars a year. (One year ago, they decided to set aside 10 percent of this revenue for Native American scholarships.)

Most faculty and administrators support the decision for ideological and practical reasons. The student body is divided. Minority groups are overjoyed, while a few students are angry and want the old name back. Most students have remained silent on the issue.

The president, alarmed at the hostile reaction to what he thought would be a popular decision and hoping soon to announce a major capital campaign, has agreed to reconsider and has asked Gabrielle, the Student Council president, to assess the views of the student body and report back in two weeks. Privately, she has learned that what the president really wants is a resolution of support. How should she proceed?

QUESTIONS TO GUIDE DISCUSSION

1. Is two weeks enough time to assess student opinion accurately? Since the Student Council is a representative body, could Gabrielle just take a vote?

2. More than thirty teams in the NCAA have American Indian nicknames. Do educational institutions have a special obligation to take a proactive leadership role in fighting prejudicial stereotypes?

3. How do you feel about team names such as the Washington Redskins, the Florida State Seminoles, the Atlanta Braves, and the Cleveland Indians? What about Notre Dame's Fighting Irish or the Hope College Flying Dutchmen? Do these names and traditions perpetuate negative stereotypes, or are they harmless?

NOW WHAT IF?

- The decision had been to keep the name but change the logo, mascot, and pregame ritual.

- Gabrielle strongly opposes the name change and privately despises the president for what she thinks was a cowardly decision.

- The president had decided to stand firm and ride out the storm instead of reopening the issue.

CASE IN POINT

Gabrielle faces a personal leadership dilemma. In trying to accommodate all parties, she risks losing her effectiveness and alienating everyone.

In *The 7 Habits of Highly Effective People*, Steven Covey isolates and analyzes the habits of effective people.

- They take initiative and responsibility based on a personal vision.

- They have a clear understanding of their personal goals.

- They act in accordance with a strong set of personal values.

- They seek solutions that are mutually satisfying and beneficial.
- They empathize with others.
- They are open to new possibilities.
- They find ways to renew themselves physically, spiritually, mentally, and socially.

He finds that these habits are actually attitudes toward self and others that facilitate constructive human interaction and lead to satisfying agreements and solutions.

Using the context of Gabrielle's problem-solving crisis at Fairfax State, develop a list of 7 habits of highly *ineffective* people—behaviors or attitudes that preclude good communication and thwart attempts at personal leadership. In other words, identify seven responses to Gabrielle's problematic situation as Student Council president that would be counterproductive to a resolution of the logo issue.

1. Do you possess any of the ineffective habits cited?
2. Is it possible to change an ineffective habit into an effective one? How?
3. How do you explain the phenomenon of enduring leaders who appear to possess some of the ineffective habits you have described?

WRITING ASSIGNMENT

As a group project, conduct a survey of student opinion, asking the following question:

> What do you think of team names and logos that depict ethnic or racial groups, such as the Marquette Warriors and the Fighting Irish of Notre Dame? Do these names promote harmful stereotypes?

Each group member should try to collect at least twenty responses. After the responses are summarized and the numerical results totaled, distribute copies to the members. Each person should then write an analysis of the survey results.

SHOWTIME

Cast of Characters

STUDENT A The chair of the Board of Regents
STUDENT B A Choctaw chief
STUDENT C A representative of the American Indian Movement (AIM)
STUDENT D The president of the Alumni Association
STUDENT E The president of the Faculty Council

STUDENT F Gabrielle
OTHERS   Members of the Board of Regents

The Plot

The boardroom.

Members of the board sit in the front row. Speakers sit at the desk in front while speaking, then return to their seats behind the board.

The board is conducting a hearing on the name change. The chair explains that even though a decision has been made, they are willing to reconsider, as the president has requested, if a sufficiently persuasive case can be made for one side or the other. Members want to hear both sides of the issue, as well as how the students feel about it.

The first speaker is a Choctaw chief, wearing typical modern American dress. He explains that only he is authorized to speak for his tribe and that the next speaker represents a radical minority held in contempt by tribal elders. The Choctaws, he says, are proud to be enshrined forever as the symbol of a great college and have benefited materially from the association. He offers to advise the college on ways to strengthen its association with the Choctaws and to eliminate stereotypical portrayals.

The delegate from AIM, dressed in traditional Native American regalia, takes the stand and speaks eloquently about conditions on the reservations, about American Indian pride, and about the harm done by negative stereotypes of American Indians. She applauds the board's courage and leadership in setting this example for other universities to follow.

The president of the Alumni Association decries the decision as having been made without consulting the alumni, an act of deceit and cowardice. She blames the president, an outsider without knowledge of or sympathy for years of tradition, for this decision. Until the Choctaw name is restored, she says, the alumni will continue to protest and withhold their support. "We are Choctaws forever," she concludes. "We will be a thorn in your side, and we will never go away!"

The president of the Faculty Council expresses the predominant faculty view, deploring racial prejudice in all forms and emphasizing the leadership role universities must assume in promoting diversity and sensitivity to minority concerns.

The final speaker is Gabrielle, who reports on the results of her survey of student opinion.

The board then meets privately to deliberate, returning in no less than five minutes to announce its final, irreversible decision and give its reasons.

RESEARCH KIT

Print/On-line Resources

- Articles/editorials on the use of ethnic mascots, logos, trademarks
- College mission statements
- Publications and Web page of AIM
- Publications of Bureau of Indian Affairs (state or federal)
- College nondiscrimination statements/policies
- Example of a resolution of support

Human Resources

- President of Native American student organization
- Coordinator of multicultural center on campus
- Athletic director
- Indian tribal officials
- College president or board member
- Public information officer at a college with current/former ethnic mascot
- Alumni association representative

The Skinhead

Virtually all the students in the residence hall expressed outrage when a swastika was spray-painted on the ground-floor window of a Jewish resident over the weekend.

Rumor has it that one of the residents, Derek, a young man who shaves his head and is notorious for his eccentric behavior, was seen that weekend at a party wearing a button that said HITLER LIVES! The outside of his door is covered with punk paraphernalia, and students who have visited his room say that it is filled with Nazi slogans and memorabilia.

Derek is a popular student in the hall. He is a talented lead singer and guitarist in a band he organized called The Third Reich. He has surrounded himself with a coterie of acolytes dressed, coifed, and tattooed in the neo-Nazi manner. Although he earns average grades, he is intelligent and creative.

Danielle, a graduate student who was pressed into duty at the last minute as hall director, confronted Derek about the spray-painting incident. He denied any involvement in it and declined to speculate on who may have been responsible. Beyond that, he refused to discuss the matter further unless specific charges were brought in a public hearing.

Danielle would like to handle this matter on her own, as quietly as possible, because she recently had to ask for help from the housing director for an alcohol problem on her floor that created negative publicity for the college. The housing director dealt with the problem but told Danielle that hall directors were paid to *prevent* crises. What are Danielle's options at this point?

QUESTIONS TO GUIDE DISCUSSION

1. What are the top three challenges Danielle faces? How would you prioritize them? How should she deal with each one? Where could she turn for help?

2. What are the limits of a hall director's authority in disciplinary cases? Should Danielle contact the campus police? Is this only a crime of vandalism or something more? How does this incident compare to a cross burning by the Ku Klux Klan?

3. Are the rights of the accused and the safety of the Jewish student equally important? Would it be fair to separate the students by moving one of them to another residence hall? What if both were unwilling to move? If so, which one should be forced to move?

NOW WHAT IF?

- The next day the Jewish student's car windows are broken. An anonymous note from an alleged eyewitness informs Danielle that Derek was the perpetrator.

- Derek has been written up several times for violations of hall rules (alcohol in his room, loud music during quiet hours, and so on).

- Derek's band, The Third Reich, is the lead band scheduled to perform next week at the Fall Fling sponsored by the Residence Hall Association.

CASE IN POINT

Although the hall director position is Danielle's first significant leadership opportunity, she is regarded by the Housing Office and her peers as a campus leader. As an authority figure in a college residence hall, Danielle is vulnerable to undermining attacks; she can expect challenges to her attempts to enforce housing regulations.

Her encounter with Derek will help shape her style as a leader and perhaps determine how she handles the pressures and expectations of leadership. The incident may even help Danielle decide whether she wants to continue to pursue a leadership track. In *Communicating,* Roy Berko, Andrew Wolvin, and Darlyn Wolvin explore the motivations of leaders. They list five basic reasons for people wanting to be leaders.

- *Information.* Many leaders enjoy having access to inside or privileged information.

- *Rewards.* Leaders receive many benefits from their positions, including praise, attention, power, privileges, and material rewards.

- *Expectations.* Certain individuals have sufficient self-confidence to believe they can pursue a given goal or solve a problem better than anyone else.
- *Acceptance.* For some, attaining a title or office means they have gained respect and acceptance.
- *Status.* Acquiring status in one group often results in status being conferred by other groups as well.

1. Can you think of other reasons people want to be leaders?
2. Are some motivations to lead more respectable or altruistic than others?
3. Does the reason a person wants to be a leader affect the style or performance of that leader?
4. If you want to be a leader, explain why.

WRITING ASSIGNMENT

Read the following memo carefully:

TO: Hall Residents

FROM: Danielle Jones
        Hall Director

RE: Snitch and Get Rich

I am just about fed up with violations of Hall Code 47 and whoever it is is going to pay through the nose if he keeps it up. That's right, you, you know who you are and if you don't know what Code 47 is look it up. I'm talking about racist garbage painted on peoples windows not to mention beer cans in the hall near your room and vomit in the communal bathrooms that the custodial staff is threatening to not clean up any more and everything that goes with it I think you know what I mean.

Starting pronto we're going to nip this thing in the bud before all you freaks all get kicked out on your fannies and I'm talking out of <u>school</u> not just out of the <u>hall</u>. Starting today we're operating on a strict honor code where if you see anything fishy going on you will report that violation to me.

Anyone who reports a Code 47 and it results in the person getting written up I will personally give the sum of $25 from the hall treasury. That's right, I'm talking about the money we WERE going to use for a new VCR, the Springlet Sniglet, the sleeping bag seminar at Lake Garibaldi, and the rock concert next spring.

The party's over, dude!!!

In your group, identify the faults of the memo and suggest ways it could be improved. Try a revision of your own, then share your draft with the group. Taking the best elements from all the revisions, prepare a final draft as a team project.

SHOWTIME

The residence hall government meets to decide what to do about Derek. Some want him kicked out of the hall immediately; others believe his right to express himself, even though his views are repugnant, should be protected at all costs. Still others believe that a proactive program is needed in the hall to educate students about anti-Semitism and hate crimes.

Danielle moderates the session with five hall government officers. The rest of the class observes and takes notes on group dynamics. After the session is concluded (fifteen to twenty minutes), observers give feedback to the officers—praising them for specific contributions, effective listening skills, problem-solving strategies, and leadership styles and offering suggestions that could make future meetings of this sort even more productive.

RESEARCH KIT ████████████████████████

Print/On-line Resources

- Residence hall contract and handbook
- Hall director job description
- College speech code
- College judicial process (nonacademic misconduct)
- Federal case law (hateful speech)

Human Resources

- Housing director
- Representative of B'nai B'rith, Chabad House, or Jewish Defense League
- American Civil Liberties Union (ACLU), private, or college attorney
- Student affairs administrator

The Price of Compassion

When Edna contracted multiple sclerosis at the age of forty-six, she was forced to quit her job as a scrub nurse. Knowing that she would someday be confined to a wheelchair, she decided to enroll at the local community college to prepare herself for a new career as a technical writer.

The college's Office of Student Services, despite a very limited budget for students with disabilities, has made what it considers to be a good-faith effort to accommodate her needs. During her first year at the college, the office provided a chair helper for ten hours a week and some assistance in the library.

Now Edna is just one year short of earning her associate's degree, but her condition has taken a turn for the worse and her need for assistance is much greater. She has requested the chair helper for twenty hours a week and a person to read her assignments aloud and do typing for three hours a night, five days a week. She also needs help getting dressed, eating, and going to the bathroom.

The Office of Student Services is sympathetic but informs Edna that it has done everything it can to assist her, citing the many other students on campus with special needs, not all of which can be met with the resources available. They are unwilling to go beyond their initial commitment.

Edna is deeply discouraged. She feels discriminated against on the basis of her age and disability. Not getting the help she needs will force her to abandon her dream of completing a college degree.

How should Edna respond to this situation? How can she proceed to ensure that the college meets her needs and that her rights are protected?

QUESTIONS TO GUIDE DISCUSSION

1. Does Edna have a case? On what basis? What is the college's legal responsibility to Edna? How can she find out what her legal rights are?

2. Does Edna have an obligation to moderate her demands in light of the college's limited budget and the needs of other students? Explain.

3. Is the likelihood of a student's completing a degree an appropriate basis for defining the level of support a college should provide to that student? Defend your answer.

NOW WHAT IF?

- Edna is failing and having to repeat more and more courses. The Student Services office staff is convinced that she will never graduate.

- Edna revealed her disability on her college application. Knowing the disease was progressive and realizing that helping her would involve tremendous expense over time, the college refused to admit her even though she was academically qualified.

- Edna is twenty years old. Or she is eighty years old.

CASE IN POINT

Just finishing college is a major challenge for Edna. But if she were to aspire to a position of leadership in her chosen field, as a person with a disability she would face an even greater hurdle. Despite the examples of Helen Keller and Franklin D. Roosevelt, it is clear that people with disabilities have a more difficult time being accepted by able followers. Discrimination on the basis of a disability has prevented many people from seeking or gaining access to leadership positions.

In the chapter titled "Leadership, Blacks, Hispanics, and Other Minorities" in *Bass and Stogdill's Handbook of Leadership,* B. M. Bass notes that few controlled studies have related physical disability to leadership performance. They note no new research in this area since 1980.

Consider the following research questions that might be studied by leadership scholars:

- How do able followers react to leaders with physical disabilities?

- What reactions by able followers reduce the success or effectiveness of leaders with disabilities?

- Are certain disabilities incompatible with leadership?

- What unique perspectives or experiences can a leader with a disability bring to an organization?

- In what ways can the personal challenge of a disability be viewed as a positive leadership trait?

Place yourself in the role of a leadership scholar who is concerned with the relationship between leadership performance and physical or mental disability. Consider the following questions:

1. In addition to the questions above, what other issues merit further study?

2. What research methodology would be best suited to answering these questions: survey research, data collection and statistical analysis, or personal interviews? What other methodologies might be used?

3. Do you feel American society is moving toward a more enlightened view on this issue? If so, what evidence can you cite?

WRITING ASSIGNMENT

Under what circumstances is a public institution *not* obliged to accommodate the demands or requests of a person with a disability? Are there cases where free physical access to educational opportunity can be denied or abridged? To answer these questions, you will need to consult three key pieces of federal legislation.

- Vocational Rehabilitation Act of 1973
- Americans with Disabilities Act of 1990
- Individuals with Disabilities Education Act of 1990

You also may want to research some of the more important cases involving the rights of persons with disabilities in an educational setting.

- *Grove City* v. *Bell* (1984)
- *Southeastern Community College* v. *Davis* (1979)
- *Wright* v. *Columbia University* (1981)

Develop one or two scenarios in which a public or private educational institution may act legally to deny special accommodation requests by persons with disabilities.

SHOWTIME

Get together in small groups (four or five students) and take turns describing a moment in your life when you became aware of a prejudice you had against a person with a physical or mental disability. How do you feel about such persons today? If you feel differently, explain what caused this change. Other group members may ask for clarification but should avoid judgmental comments or advice.

RESEARCH KIT

Print/On-line Resources

- Americans with Disabilities Act and articles on its implications for higher education
- College policy on rights of students with disabilities
- College admissions procedures
- Student handbook
- Articles on college students with disabilities

Human Resources

- Representative of Student Services Office
- Student who is chair bound
- Admissions Office staff member
- Medical doctor
- Attorney specializing in disabled rights or college attorney

Black Is White

Professor Black had been heavily recruited by the African American studies department at Warner University as an expert in African history. He was hired on the strength of his emerging reputation as an award-winning teacher at a major university in the Pacific Northwest, his impressive record of grants and publications, and his active role in the local chapter of the National Association for the Advancement of Colored People (NAACP). But when he arrived on campus, it became apparent that he lacked one major credential: Professor Black was white.

Every seat was filled for his first class on African colonialism, but when Dr. Black walked in, most of the students walked out.

The seats were filled again for the second class—this time with twice as many students, some enrolled and some not, many of them chanting slogans and waving signs that read:

BLACK FACULTY FOR BLACK STUDIES

PROFESSOR BLACK JUST DOESN'T GET IT

BROTHERS ONLY NEED APPLY

The protesters, led by an enrolled student named Mustafa X, made it clear that they would continue to disrupt the class until Dr. Black was replaced by a person of color.

Dr. Black attempted to reason with the protesters, but to no avail. Speaking for them, Mustafa X explained that a white person could not possibly understand the experience of people of color and was therefore unqualified to teach them. Moreover, he said, the text Professor Black had selected for the class contained inaccurate information: it failed, for example, to point out that Jews were responsible for the slave trade. When Dr. Black responded that such claims were nonsense, he was shouted down amid calls for a *jihad*, or holy war.

Finding it impossible to proceed, he took his case to the department head, who enforced university policy by having Mr. X forcibly removed from the class. This action led to a silent protest by the Black Student Alliance (BSA), members of which arrived early and filled every seat, forcing enrolled students to stand in the back. Mr. X had notified the electronic media of this event. In a televised interview shown on the evening news, he called the department head an "Oreo" and warned that "the campus is about to explode."

The dean, frightened by this turn of events, reinstated Mr. X and agreed to allow the silent protest as long as the number of students in the room did not exceed fire code requirements. Dr. Black refused to teach under these circumstances. As a result, he was fired and replaced by a part-time lecturer.

Dr. Black has since filed suit with the American Civil Liberties Union (ACLU) for reinstatement and damages. He also is asking students, especially students of color, to take a leadership role in protesting his firing.

If you were a student leader at Warner, how would you respond?

QUESTIONS TO GUIDE DISCUSSION

1. What is the core problem here? What is the critical situation that needs to be rectified in the short term? In the long term?

2. Do the protesters have a legitimate complaint? What could Professor Black, the department head, the dean, and the protesters have done differently to resolve the conflict? Which group has the strongest motivation to do so?

3. Are race, ethnicity, gender, sexual orientation, religion, age, or marital status legitimate hiring criteria? Are some legitimate and others not? If these are unacceptable criteria, what strategies could a hiring authority use to diversify its work force?

NOW WHAT IF?

- A male instructor had been hired to teach women's studies.
- The dean had enforced Warner University policy and called in the campus police to remove the protesters.
- Dr. Black's suit is successful, and he is reinstated in the class by court order.

CASE IN POINT

In one sense, Professor Black could be viewed as a victim of ineffective academic leadership. The administrators at Warner missed an opportunity to turn the incident into a positive learning experience for everyone involved. Instead, the campus was disrupted, racial tension was exacerbated, and Dr. Black's career was placed in jeopardy.

What criteria distinguish effective academic leadership from average or poor performance in this area? Consider the following description of an effective academic leader:

- Articulates a defined vision of institutional goals and priorities
- Creates an atmosphere and culture that promotes learning
- Is a visible presence and influence in the institution
- Monitors instructor and student performance
- Personally exemplifies the highest standards of teaching and scholarship

1. Identify additional criteria to measure the effectiveness of college leaders.
2. Prioritize all the criteria, including your own, with the most important measure of effective leadership listed first.
3. What expressions of leadership could have prevented or moderated the incident with Professor Black?

WRITING ASSIGNMENT

Pretend you are Professor Black. Compose five entries in a journal format (about one hundred words per entry) that reflect the professor's private reactions to the following course of events during his short, unhappy service at Warner University:

(Day One) Professor Black walks in; the students walk out.

(Day Two) The students demonstrate with signs and chant insulting slogans.

(Day Three) Professor Black attempts to reason with the students outside of class.

(Day Four) Professor Black is challenged by students regarding his textbook.

(Day Five) The BSA stages a silent protest and sit-in, disrupting his class.

SHOWTIME

Facing the media is a job many leaders dread, but it is an important skill and one that can be learned with practice.

Conduct a press conference featuring the principal characters in this case. First, select volunteers to play the parts of the dean of arts and sciences, the head of the African American Studies Department, Professor Black, Mustafa X, the president of the Black Faculty and Staff Association, and the ACLU attorney representing Professor Black. The six actors are interviewed in succession—singly, not as a group.

The other class members function as reporters. Each should prepare six tough questions in advance—one for each of the six interviewees. Each class member should have an opportunity to ask at least one question.

When the interviews are over, discuss how the actors handled the questions. What techniques were most effective? What were you trying to accomplish as an interviewer? What are some appropriate objectives for an interviewee? How would you have answered your own questions?

If possible, videotape the interviews. Then have the actors critique their own responses and body language.

RESEARCH KIT

Print/On-line Resources

- College speech code
- Faculty recruitment and hiring practices and affirmative action guidelines
- American Association of University Professors (AAUP) statement on academic freedom
- African American Studies Department mission statement and department bulletin
- ACLU position statements
- Articles on Afrocentrism
- Articles on reverse discrimination and racial credentialing

Human Resources

- NAACP official
- African American studies director
- Dean (humanities/social sciences)
- ACLU attorney
- Director of human resources/personnel office
- Faculty union spokesperson

The Homophobe

Danny is a gay student who lives on the floor of the residence hall where Rashid recently began his new job as resident adviser. Someone has tacked an unsigned poster on Danny's door. The message is painfully brief:

AIDS IS NOT THE PROBLEM.

GAYS ARE THE PROBLEM.

AIDS IS THE SOLUTION.

This is the third time this incident has occurred since the semester began three weeks ago—each time a different message with a homophobic theme. Other residents—some gay, lesbian, or bisexual and others heterosexual—have received similar messages and discussed them with fellow residents. Many have expressed their concern to Rashid. Most claim to know who did it. Danny is outraged and has threatened reprisals against the rumored offender unless Rashid does something about it.

Rashid is hesitant to take action against the alleged offender, who is an honors student active in hall government and the designer of last year's prize-winning homecoming float. But he needs to do something, and fast. The tension is thick, and rumors are spreading like wildfire. What should he do?

QUESTIONS TO GUIDE DISCUSSION

1. What is the best way to resolve an interpersonal conflict based on different lifestyles and sexual orientations?

2. Does the inflammatory, even threatening, nature of the poster suggest more than merely protesting another person's sexual orientation? Can this be construed as a criminal act?

3. Some people object strongly to homosexuality. What is the nature of their argument, and how do you assess its assumptions and logic?

Assuming the harasser holds such assumptions, would Rashid be wise to engage the student in debate on the subject?

NOW WHAT IF?

▪ The poster had appeared on bulletin boards in the lounge instead of on the student's door.

▪ The poster had been signed.

▪ The message had been mailed to the student.

CASE IN POINT

Rashid's leadership skills as resident adviser will be seriously tested. He is confronted with representatives from both sides of the issue, and the situation could get out of control. His initial leadership strategy must be decisive; there is little time to deliberate or consult.

When confronted by a crisis, leaders face special challenges. The following behaviors are recognized in leadership studies as characteristic of a leader who is effective under pressure:

▪ Remains poised

▪ Keeps information flowing and communication channels open

▪ Offers clear contingency plans

▪ Focuses on the specifics of the problem or issue

▪ Is willing to go beyond the protocols of stated authority

▪ Remains committed to group or organizational goals

1. What other actions would facilitate positive outcomes for a leader in a crisis situation?

2. What are the most critical steps Rashid can take to be effective in this volatile situation? Is it already too late for him to take some of these steps?

3. Do you consider yourself to be effective under pressure? What are some of your most constructive responses to such situations? What actions have you taken in crises? Were they effective?

WRITING ASSIGNMENT

What is homophobia? Research the concept and summarize what you learn. What is the origin of the term? To what specific behaviors does it apply? How pervasive is homophobia in American society? In other societies? Do some cultures condone homophobic attitudes more than others? Are some societies more tolerant than others of homosexuality? Conclude with a statement about your own attitude toward homophobic individuals or behaviors.

SHOWTIME

Before any discussion of this case, the facilitator should copy, distribute, and collect the confidential survey on page 86. Participation in the survey should be completely voluntary, and those who choose to participate must be guaranteed absolute privacy and confidentiality.

After discussion of the case is concluded, the facilitator shares the survey results with the class. Subsequent class discussion should focus on the following questions:

- Are the survey results consistent with the opinions expressed during class discussion?
- Do students feel differently about the questions now that they have discussed the case?
- In what ways have opinions changed?
- If the survey results are consistent with views expressed in class, how did class discussion reinforce those views?

SURVEY					
	Strongly Agree	Agree	Unsure/ No Comment	Disagree	Strongly Disagree
1. Homosexual activity is morally wrong.					
2. I am heterosexual.					
3. I have friends or relatives who are gay, lesbian, or bisexual.					
4. I think a person's sexuality should be kept private.					
5. AIDS is God's way of punishing the sin of homosexuality.					
6. I think it's important for people in the closet to come out.					
7. I have taken active steps to show my support for gays, lesbians, and bisexuals.					
8. I have been the object of unwelcome homosexual advances.					
9. Homosexuality is a distasteful subject that I would prefer to avoid.					
10. Homophobia is the major obstacle to finding a cure for AIDS.					

RESEARCH KIT

Print/On-line Resources

- College speech code
- College policies/statements on rights of persons who are gay, lesbian, or bisexual
- Residence hall contract and housing handbook
- Job description—resident adviser
- Federal civil rights and nondiscrimination statutes
- Articles on homophobia

Human Resources

- Residence hall director
- Representative of gay/lesbian/bisexual student or faculty organization
- Psychologist or psychology instructor
- Counseling Office staff member

A Celebration of Whiteness

For the past twenty years, certain special-interest groups on campus (Hispanics, African Americans, Native Americans, women, and gay/lesbian/bisexual students) have been encouraged to celebrate their identity and traditions by means of a special week, usually featuring celebrity speakers, exhibits, and a capstone event such as a banquet, march, dance, fiesta, or powwow. Each of these groups may apply for up to five thousand dollars per year from a subaccount in the student government treasury of twenty thousand dollars. All groups get the same amount based on the total number of requests.

A group of white students (many of them student leaders) have formally proposed that similar recognition be accorded to them in the form of White Male Week.

"This is not a joke," they pointed out in a presentation to student government officers. "We demand the same rights as any other special-interest group on campus." If their request is not approved, they will announce plans to agitate for the abolition of all special weeks for minorities and special-interest groups.

Barbara is an elected member of student government. How should she vote on this proposal? Is there anything she can do or say in the meeting that might turn this potentially divisive controversy into an opportunity for constructive dialogue?

QUESTIONS TO GUIDE DISCUSSION

1. Would the establishment of a white male week unify or divide your own campus? Explain.
2. If the proposal were approved, do you think the white students would seriously begin planning a weeklong schedule of meaningful cultural events or lose interest, having made their point?

3. Have white males been left out of the national debate on civil rights and affirmative action? Is it possible that there is some real pain behind this proposal?

NOW WHAT IF?

- The proposal was not approved, and the white students made good on their promise, with the result that all special-interest weeks were outlawed.

- The proposal was approved, with the result that one special-interest group after another—students with disabilities, veterans, commuters, adult students, even the lacrosse team—sought and won approval and financial support for a special week in their honor.

- After the white students finished their presentation, a female member of student government said, "White Male Week? Get real! You've already got fifty-two of them."

CASE IN POINT

The issue facing the campus is volatile and serious. Barbara and other members of student government will need to promote a discussion that defuses the tension and leads to positive dialogue. In *Stewardship*, Peter Block delineates the concept of stewardship as a nontraditional way to exercise leadership and to use power so that service to the well-being of the group is paramount. According to Block, organizations should be redesigned on the basis of stewardship with a strong sense of partnership and shared purpose. He notes four requirements that need to be present to have a real partnership.

- *Exchange of purpose.* Everyone is responsible for defining vision and values.
- *Right to say no.* Dissenting ideas must be heard.
- *Joint accountability.* Outcomes and quality of cooperation are everyone's responsibility.
- *Absolute honesty.* Not telling the truth is an act of betrayal.

1. Which of these partnership principles will be important for Barbara and the others members of student government during their discussions? Why?

2. How can the focus on partnership and shared purpose help resolve the issue that divides the campus?

3. What are the advantages of a stewardship/partnership approach to leadership? Are there situations where such an approach would be a disadvantage?

WRITING ASSIGNMENT

Prepare a two-page proposal to student government outlining the principal arguments for White Male Week. Include a sample schedule of events. Your proposal should be a serious one, free of irony and sarcasm.

OR

Prepare a two-page proposal to replace all culture-specific weeks with a campus-wide Celebration of Diversity, a weeklong series of events designed to promote intercultural understanding.

SHOWTIME

Meet in small groups.

Before discussion begins, take a moment to list up to three cultures that you consider most important to understanding who you are (for example, female, Asian American, Roman Catholic). Make a second list of the subcultures to which you belong (for example, martial artist, Internet surfer, morris dancer, bridge fanatic).

Take turns reading these lists aloud to the group. Were your lists mostly similar or different? How many different cultures and subcultures were represented by the entire group?

RESEARCH KIT

Print/On-line Resources

- Student affairs/campus life policy on campuswide events
- Student government policies and procedures
- Student handbook
- Planning/program documents (special-interest events)
- Articles on history of discrimination against minorities

Human Resources

- Ethnic studies directors
- Representatives of minority interest groups
- Student affairs administrator (student life)
- Minority community leaders

PART FOUR

Leadership and Group Dynamics

Creating unity in the midst of diversity; orchestrating a mixed chorus of stakeholders and individual needs within a small group or a large organization; reconciling opposing views and resolving conflicts; mobilizing people toward a common goal—these are perhaps the most difficult challenges student leaders face.

The Smoldering Volcano

After a year of excitement as the winner of a statewide science fair, Candace has enrolled as a scholarship student at Pine Ridge Community College. She is one of a select few who will live in the college's only residence hall. In two years, she expects to transfer to the state university. She has always been proud of her ability to manage her life and control her destiny, but now her fate seems to be in the hands of others.

Her earth science instructor has divided the class into teams of four. Each team is supposed to get together outside of class as often as necessary to prepare a group project on various natural phenomena. Since each group member will receive the same grade for the quality of the group presentation, it is important that everyone contributes equally.

Candace is excited about her group project dealing with volcanoes. She has a lot of ideas that will require a great deal of work, such as constructing an actual functioning volcano that bubbles, smokes, and finally erupts as the group concludes its presentation.

She volunteers as group leader and arranges the first meeting, assigning each of the other three group members a task to perform or an item to bring to the meeting. Unfortunately, things don't go quite as planned. Juwon, a commuting student, arrives half an hour late due to a traffic jam on the interstate. Estelle, an older student, arrives on time but is unprepared because she is exhausted from working nights and has had no time to turn her attention to the project. And Boon Lee, a Malaysian American student, thinks Candace's erupting volcano idea is ridiculous. He believes their first priority should be to research the topic thoroughly and make a formal presentation based on good science.

As their presentation date approaches, Candace is in despair. Juwon has taken a casual approach to the work and laughingly dismisses Candace's mother-hen attitude. Estelle has continued to procrastinate, although she assures Candace that her part will be done well. Boon Lee has done an amazing amount of research, but Candace is afraid that if he dominates the presentation, the class will be bored stiff.

Candace is tempted to abandon her role as group leader and try to persuade the instructor to let her make a solo presentation. Is this a good idea? With one week to go, what advice would you give her?

QUESTIONS TO GUIDE DISCUSSION

1. How would Candace benefit by a better understanding of the differences among the members of her group?

2. Why are empowering, enabling, and delegating considered important leadership skills? Why are leaders sometimes reluctant to delegate tasks to followers?

3. If you were the instructor, would you make an exception for Candace and allow her to make a solo presentation? Why or why not?

NOW WHAT IF?

▪ Candace decides to resign as group leader and to ask one of the others to take over.

▪ The instructor uses peer grading, where each group member evaluates the contributions of all the other members of the group.

▪ Candace makes a solo presentation but receives a lower grade than any of the groups.

CASE IN POINT

As group leader, Candace faces a daunting challenge. She needs to motivate the group, facilitate organized class presentations, and create a sense of teamwork and cooperation.

The following eleven principles of army leadership[1] are regarded by the U.S. armed forces as essential characteristics of leaders of organized, team-oriented military activities. Examine these principles in relation to Candace's civilian problem.

---

[1] Department of the Army, *Military Leadership*, FM-22-100, July 1990.

- Know yourself and seek self-improvement.
- Be tactically and technically proficient.
- Seek responsibility and take responsibility for your actions.
- Make sound and timely decisions.
- Set the example.
- Know your soldiers and look out for their well-being.
- Keep your subordinates informed.
- Develop a sense of responsibility in your subordinates.
- Ensure that the task is understood, supervised, and accomplished.
- Build the team.
- Employ your unit in accordance with its capabilities.

1. Which of these principles of army leadership could Candace use effectively?
2. Are there any principles here that do not apply to the context of Candace's classroom?
3. Which of the principles of army leadership apply equally to civilian culture? Which are unique to the military? Explain.

WRITING ASSIGNMENT

What leadership skills does Candace need to bring out the best in each group member? List five of them. Then create a "to do" list for Candace that contains five specific tasks (related to each of the five leadership skills) that she can do to reorganize or redirect her nonproductive group.

SHOWTIME

This activity requires prior planning and at least one rehearsal.

Two teams in the class are getting together for the first time to plan their presentations. (Team A's topic is lightning; Team B's topic is tornadoes.)

Reconstruct their initial planning sessions (each enactment should take no more than ten minutes), with Team A illustrating ineffective group behaviors and Team B illustrating effective ones.

Afterward, the audience should comment on the leadership styles and small-group dynamics—both effective and ineffective—that they observed in the reenactments.

RESEARCH KIT

Print/On-line Resources

- A small-group communication text
- An intercultural communication text
- Books and articles on group dynamics and team building (see Selected Bibliography)
- Articles on collaborative learning
- Your college's grade-grievance procedure
- Statement of student rights

Human Resources

- Any head/chair of an academic department
- Faculty member (speech communication, intercultural, and/or small group)
- Expert in collaborative learning (teacher education department)
- College dean or academic vice president

The Rockdale Scandal

Some months ago, an enterprising reporter for a major newspaper wrote a sensational article about cheating in college. Most of the research for the article was done at Rockdale College, where the reporter had disguised his identity and posed as a student for an entire semester. The article claimed that 77 percent of all students at Rockdale cheat on tests, a claim that is supported by survey data and anecdotal evidence. Unfortunately, the article was picked up by a national wire service, with the result that the college's public image is now in tatters.

In an attempt to redeem the college's tarnished reputation (Rockdale was already known as a "jock school"), the administration is proposing a tough new anticheating policy that emphasizes dire punishments for anyone caught cheating. Instructors would be required to attend workshops on how to detect and prevent cheating. As a final step before the new policy is approved, the proposal has been submitted to the Educational Policies Committee of the college board, on which Gary is the student representative.

Like most of the students he has talked to, Gary considers the policy punitive and probably ineffective. Faculty leaders have insisted that attendance at workshops must be strictly voluntary. Still, he knows cheating has become a serious problem at his school and something has to be done. Privately, some board members have politely suggested that student leaders "put up or shut up." In other words, "if you don't think this plan will work, give us something that will."

Gary, a marketing major, has three weeks to develop an alternative proposal for presentation before the Educational Policies Committee. What kind of proposal would satisfy the committee, the students, and the faculty? What strategies could he use to obtain support from these three groups?

QUESTIONS TO GUIDE DISCUSSION

1. What conditions would Gary's proposal need to meet to satisfy the various constituencies at Rockdale College?

2. What are the fundamental reasons for cheating? What changes could be made at your school that would remove or reduce the motivation to cheat?

3. Some colleges—Rhodes College, Duke University, the military academies—have honor systems to guard against cheating. Does your college have an honor system? If not, how could you find out more about such systems—how they work and how effective they are? Would an honor system work at your college? Why or why not?

NOW WHAT IF?

▨ Gary himself occasionally cheats on tests.

▨ Privately, Gary hates cheating and agrees with the proposed policy, but most of the students he represents disapprove of the policy.

▨ Gary's girlfriend has been accused of cheating. If she is found guilty, her punishment would be much more severe under the new policy.

CASE IN POINT

Like many young leaders, Gary is in the process of developing a personal leadership style. During such a learning process, there are many actions and responses that could thwart his attempts to lead.

Examine the following factors that frequently cause problems for would-be leaders as cited in *Off the Track: Why and How Successful Executives Get Derailed* by M. W. McCall and M. M. Lombardo:

▨ Insensitive or abrasive style

▨ Self-centered ambition

▨ Inability to select good subordinates

▨ Inability to take a long-term perspective

▨ Aloofness or arrogance

▨ Betrayal of someone's trust

1. Are some of these factors more likely than others to derail Gary's efforts?

2. Have you observed any of these behaviors in leaders you have encountered?

3. What historical figures have been derailed as leaders because they exhibited some of these behaviors?

4. Are any of these factors at work in your attempts to be a leader?

WRITING ASSIGNMENT

Write a letter to the editor of your campus paper expressing your views on the proposed policy. Here are some guidelines:

- *Be positive.* If you oppose the get-tough approach, offer a better alternative.

- *Be brief.* Pretend the newspaper charges letter writers ten cents a word.

- *Be specific.* Use concrete language, factual details, and examples.

Make copies of your rough draft for members of your group and respond to their suggestions in your revision. [Alternative: Write about a real issue on your campus, then mail the letter to the editor of your campus newspaper.]

SHOWTIME

Six volunteers sit in a circle in the center of the room for a problem-solving session. Other class members sit around the perimeter, observing and taking notes on the group's dynamics. The task for the central group is to come up with an alternative policy promoting academic integrity at Rockdale. The task for the observers is to assess the effectiveness of the problem-solving process.

The group should spend at least ten minutes (more if time permits) on each of the three major phases of the critical-thinking process.

1. Defining the problem
2. Brainstorming solutions
3. Choosing the best solution

Each phase will have a different group leader. (Students may volunteer for this role or be appointed by the facilitator-timekeeper.)

When the process is complete (about thirty minutes), the balance of the session should be used to analyze group dynamics. What leadership styles were used by the group leaders, and how effective were they? How effective was the process in achieving consensus? What were the obstacles to the group's success? How might the process have been improved?

RESEARCH KIT

Print/On-line Resources

- Honor codes/academic misconduct policies of other colleges (many available on the World Wide Web)
- Your own college's student handbook and conduct code
- College judicial process for academic misconduct
- Articles on academic misconduct (library search)
- Example of a successful proposal (any subject)

Human Resources

- Board member
- Dean of students or vice president for student affairs
- Academic dean or vice president
- Television or newspaper reporter
- College attorney
- Member of faculty Educational Policies Committee

At Your Service

At its next monthly meeting, the Faculty Senate will vote on a proposal that states, "All students who begin college this fall will be required to complete 100 hours of community service prior to graduation."

Since currently enrolled students are not affected, there has been little in the way of organized student protest except by a highly conservative group of undergraduates. The Rush Party, as they call themselves, refers to the proposal as the "Unemancipation Proclamation" and is threatening to mount a smear campaign against any student senator who supports a community service graduation requirement.

As president of the Student Senate at this small liberal arts college, Dianne has mixed feelings about the proposed requirement. She has done plenty of volunteer work herself and knows what a valuable learning experience it can be. But she also believes strongly that community service should be voluntary; requiring it yields grudging compliance and may even be a violation of the Thirteenth Amendment.

To obtain student input that will help them reach a decision on the proposal, the Faculty Senate has asked the Student Senate, which consists of twelve senators, for a motion to endorse or repudiate it. Three senators support the proposal, three oppose it, and the others could swing either way. Patrick, the vice president and a close friend of Dianne's, supports the proposal because he wants to be named coordinator of the new Community Service Office, a salaried position that the proposal would create.

What position should Dianne take publicly on this issue, if any? What strategies should she use to influence the outcome of the vote?

QUESTIONS TO GUIDE DISCUSSION

1   Is it Dianne's responsibility, as president and chair, to take a strictly neutral position on issues of this sort? Should effective leaders keep their

own views to themselves and confine their role to helping others understand the issues and make their own judgments?

2. What are Dianne's responsibilities to her friend Patrick? Are there situations where leaders need to suppress their personal loyalties in favor of the common good? Is this one of them?

3. Should community service be a requirement? Would offering incentives for service be a better approach? As a group, can you think of three effective ways of encouraging community service?

NOW WHAT IF?

▪ The twelve senators have already made up their minds: they support the proposal, mainly because it looks good and won't affect them anyway. Dianne strongly opposes it.

▪ Although Dianne and a majority of the senators originally supported the proposal, some of the senators have been changing their position. Dianne suspects this is due to intimidation tactics by the Rush Party.

▪ Although Dianne opposes the proposed policy, the vice president for student affairs, who strongly supports it, has been pressuring Dianne to support it, hinting that, if she does, he might provide funding for the new student government office Dianne has been wanting.

CASE IN POINT

Although Dianne herself is undecided on the issue of mandatory community service, as president she will need to help resolve disagreements and facilitate a responsible discussion by the student senators. Her management, communication, and leadership skills will be rigorously tested.

Leaders often face contentious debates and volatile group dynamics. In such situations, they need to remember and practice the following skills and behaviors:

▪ Separate the person from the issue.
▪ Invent multiple options.
▪ Maintain a professional climate.
▪ Stress organizational needs and outcomes.
▪ Encourage input from all participants.
▪ Facilitate consensus.

1. What else should Dianne do to ensure a constructive group discussion on this issue?

2. What leadership skills will she need to exhibit if the group appears hopelessly deadlocked or at odds?

3. Are there circumstances where otherwise effective leaders fail to resolve group conflict? Under what circumstances might this occur? What are the leader's options at that point?

WRITING ASSIGNMENT

As a group project, develop a proposal for community service at your college. Your proposal should address at least the following questions:

1. What is the mission of the program? What are its specific goals?

2. Is community service required or optional? If optional, what incentives will be offered?

3. What qualifies as community service? For example, will church work qualify? How about paid work? Can the service take place on campus? Can it be required as part of a course? How does service differ from professional development (e.g., internships, student teaching)?

4. How many hours of service will be required? How will the quantity and quality of the service be verified? Who will be responsible for verifying and evaluating the service performed?

5. Are any students exempted from the policy? Which ones, and why? How will faculty and staff be affected by the policy, if at all?

6. Who will benefit, and how?

7. How much will the program cost? Will the college provide transportation to and from the service site? How will the program be administered, and what will be the source of funding? Provide a detailed annual budget for the program.

In an appendix, describe the conflicts, if any, that arose in your group as you developed your plan and how these conflicts were resolved.

SHOWTIME

Act out the Student Senate meeting at which the proposal is discussed and voted on. Dianne presides. Each of the twelve student senators should have one minute to speak on the issue, followed by a secret-ballot vote. Patrick may speak but not vote. In the event of a tie, Dianne will cast the tie-breaking vote. If this occurs, she should take one minute to explain her decision.

RESEARCH KIT

Print/On-line Resources

- Community service requirements at any college (search college catalogs) and in high schools
- Your college's mission statement
- Promotional material of volunteer organizations
- Articles on community service requirements and academic service learning programs

Human Resources

- Coordinator of a community service program (required or voluntary) or academic service learning program
- Dean of students or director of student life
- Academic dean or vice president
- AmeriCorps director or student volunteer
- President of student body
- Other students, including older adults working full- or part-time

Trapped

Tanya remembers being thrilled two years ago when she was offered a position in the basement of the library tracing lost books. It paid only a little above minimum wage, but jobs were scarce, the work seemed interesting, and her parents weren't helping her with tuition.

A few student employees warned her about her boss, Mr. Peck, the circulation librarian. "Three girls have quit already," one said. "You'll be number four."

On her first day at work, she could feel him staring at her. On the second day, he made the following remarks, which made her feel uncomfortable:

"Isn't your skirt a little short?"

"I'll bet the boys like that blouse."

"I like to sleep in the nude—how about you?"

On the third day, he offered to help her carry a box of books and "accidentally" brushed the side of her breast with his hand. Tanya gave him a look, and he backed off.

A week later, the remarks began again—an off-color joke here, a double-entendre there. When he started to call her honey, Tanya decided to confront him.

"Mr. Peck," she said, "I really need this job, but I feel very uncomfortable when you make these sexual references. Can't we just maintain a professional relationship?"

"Listen, babe," he answered, "I've got a waiting list a mile long for your job. If my girls cooperate, I take care of them. Six-fifty, seven-fifty an hour, no problem. Arrive late, leave early, no problem. But if you're unhappy—hey, there's the door."

Tanya took it. For weeks she reflected on the incident and considered her options. Finally, she decided to act by forming the Student Women's

Action Team (SWAT). She declared herself president and wrote a terse mission statement: "Wage war on men!"

SWAT has been in existence for a year, and Tanya is discouraged. Its monthly meetings are poorly attended and consist mostly of angry talk and little action. Tanya has repeatedly applied for recognition as an official campus organization but refuses to submit the required constitution and bylaws because SWAT's mission statement has been judged unacceptable by the (male) dean of students.

Now, however, she has an opportunity to mobilize the group for action. Mr. Peck has struck again, and his victim, Elaine, has asked SWAT to help her file a harassment claim. How should Tanya proceed in a way that will help Elaine and all the other victims of Mr. Peck, while at the same time galvanizing SWAT into an effective student organization?

QUESTIONS TO GUIDE DISCUSSION

1. Does your institution have a formal policy on sexual harassment? Does the policy cover students? What are the procedures for filing a grievance?

2. Why has SWAT failed to become a viable student organization? How can this failure be attributed to Tanya's leadership behavior? If she has made mistakes, are they now reversible? Explain.

3. Mr. Peck's treatment of women is clearly offensive, but has he committed a criminal offense? If SWAT files a grievance against Mr. Peck and he is found guilty, what would be an appropriate penalty?

NOW WHAT IF?

▨   SWAT files a successful grievance on Elaine's behalf and she gets her job back, but Mr. Peck is still her boss.

▨   Mr. Peck takes another job out of state before the women have a chance to file a claim against him.

▨   The harassed student is a man, and his boss is a woman.

CASE IN POINT

Women who aspire to leadership roles continue to face obstacles and constraints that prevent them from realizing their full leadership potential. Leadership research has isolated a number of barriers that impede the progress of women leaders. In *Leadership: A Communication Perspective,* Michael Hackman and Craig Johnson list some of these barriers:

- *Socialization.* Through socialization, leadership comes to be viewed as the province of males. Many jobs are seen as open to men but closed to women.

- *Low self-confidence.* Low self-esteem can work to prevent women from competing for leadership positions or viewing themselves as leaders.

- *Gender role stereotypes.* Gender bias can result in positions being defined in male terms and in evaluators giving higher leadership ratings for male performance.

- *Tokenism.* As token representatives of their social group in the workplace, women tend to become isolated and to play stereotyped roles that preclude leadership consideration.

- *Biased evaluation.* When women succeed, the success is attributed to good effort, motivation, or luck; conversely, evaluators attribute successful male performance to superior ability.

- *Mentor shortage.* There are too few female mentors available to assist in the development of aspiring female leaders.

1. What other barriers for women leaders can you identify?

2. Are the obstacles that Hackman and Johnson identify equally valid or applicable? How would you rank them from most significant to least significant? Explain your ranking.

3. Do basic biological differences between men and women have any bearing on leadership potential or effectiveness? Which differences? What bearing do they have?

4. How would you characterize the current status of women as leaders in the United States? In the world?

WRITING ASSIGNMENT

Research any sexual harassment policies that may be in place at your institution. Describe the essential features of the policies. What constitutes sexual harassment? What are the procedures for filing a complaint? What protections are provided for the complainant's privacy? What protections are provided for the accused? What judicial procedures exist for a determination of guilt or innocence? What remedies are provided for the victim? What are the disciplinary procedures in cases of proven guilt?

SHOWTIME

What if Tanya had confronted Mr. Peck instead of walking out the door? Reenact two possible versions of the scene. In Version A, Tanya focuses exclusively on Mr. Peck and the behaviors she finds threatening and offensive. In Version B, she focuses on her own feelings when she is not treated with respect. Afterward, discuss the two versions. Which approach was more effective? Why? How did Mr. Peck's response differ in the two versions? Did the actor playing Tanya feel better about one approach than the other? Did the actor playing Mr. Peck prefer one approach over the other?

RESEARCH KIT

Print/On-line Resources

- College sexual harassment policy and grievance/appeal procedures
- Student and faculty handbooks
- Articles on sexual harassment
- Applicable federal/state law
- Title VII of 1964 Civil Rights Act dealing with employment

Human Resources

- Director of student employment or human resources staff member
- Counseling Office staff member
- Dean of students
- College attorney
- Faculty member or director of women's studies

Worlds Apart

As a member of student government, Gil has been asked to chair the new Multicultural Task Force charged with creating a more tolerant racial climate among student groups—an issue high on the agenda of the new student body president. Gil has thought about running for president next year and sees the task force as a golden opportunity to make a name for himself on campus and gain the support of the current student leadership.

The student body is richly diverse, but the campus is becoming increasingly Balkanized: whether it's the dining commons, the classroom, the basketball arena, fraternities and sororities, or the student union, students seem to cluster together on the basis of race, nationality, and ethnicity.

The college administration has adopted policies that albeit unintentionally, encourage the self-segregation of groups with a particular cultural identity. For example, the Student Activities Office sponsors a Take Back the Night rally and march in which men are not allowed to participate. And there's a special residence hall for international students, the W. E. B. Du Bois Center for African American students, and a lounge for feminists called WomynSpace.

Some students believe that this approach has contributed to feelings of self-esteem, solidarity, and peer support among groups that have suffered discrimination in the past. Others think that the administration is simply caving in to the political demands of special-interest groups.

What, if anything, can Gil and the Multicultural Task Force do to break down this spirit of separateness and bring men and women of different races and cultures together in a spirit of harmony?

QUESTIONS TO GUIDE DISCUSSION

1. What special leadership challenges does Gil face in trying to create a more tolerant racial climate on his campus?

2. Are Gil's political motives likely to help or harm the efforts of the task force?

3. Is voluntary segregation necessarily undesirable? What benefits do students with a common background derive from sticking together? What harm does self-segregation cause? Is the goal of racial and cultural integration, which inspired the civil rights movement of the 1960s, an outmoded ideal?

NOW WHAT IF?

▨ As Latinos, Gil and his friends have noticed that the administration has made no special accommodations for Hispanic American students— mainly, he supposes, because they have not held rallies or made demands, as the other groups have done with great success.

▨ Gil has a lot of good ideas, but they all cost money, and he has been given no budget.

▨ Gil puts out a call for volunteers to serve on the task force, but the people who respond are either not very capable or are people he personally dislikes.

CASE IN POINT

In leading the Multicultural Task Force, Gil is likely to encounter the same spirit of separateness that afflicts the entire campus. His immediate challenge is to establish a cooperative dialogue among task force members that will resemble the consensus and interaction he hopes will develop in the broader university population.

In their 1989 text *Teamwork,* Carl Larson and Frank LaFasto identified the following strategies as essential to successful group dynamics and team building:

▨ Establish clear team goals.

▨ Assemble competent team members.

▨ Strive for unified commitment.

- Set up a collaborative environment.
- Encourage standards of excellence.
- Furnish support and recognition.

1. What are the most important team-building goals and outcomes that Gil should aspire to in his role as chair?
2. What other constructive behaviors could Gil exhibit to help the task force function as a team?
3. Evaluate your performance as a team member. In what ways have you been successful or resistant in this role?

WRITING ASSIGNMENT

Develop a written proposal for an innovative, campus-wide activity designed to promote multicultural and multiracial harmony. Describe specific features of the activity and indicate how the interaction of all groups will be achieved. Attach a line-item budget limited to five dollars per participant (that is, if the activity will involve five hundred people, your budget will be twenty-five hundred dollars).

SHOWTIME

Get together in small groups and develop a plan of action for creating a pluralistic campus community that will be a national model for multicultural and multiracial harmony. Agree on specific features of the plan and indicate how the interaction of all groups will be achieved. You have twenty-five thousand dollars to work with. Develop a line-item budget for your plan.

Choose a member of your group to present your plan to the entire class. The class should provide feedback on each plan based on its likely effectiveness in achieving harmony among the different cultures represented on campus. Which group is likely to get the most bang for its buck?

RESEARCH KIT

Print/On-line Resources

- Dalton, *Racial Healing* (New York: Doubleday, 1986)
- Articles on self-segregation (voluntary segregation)
- Brochures and program statements of special-interest fraternities and sororities and other campus organizations
- College mission statement and policies on diversity
- Research on retention/persistence to graduation of minority college students

Human Resources

- Coordinator of multicultural center
- Dean of students
- Spokesperson for an African American fraternity or sorority
- Representative from housing/dining services
- Sociology or intercultural communications instructor
- Ethnic studies director

The Package Is Ticking

A local packaging magnate, C. B. "Hoss" Pickens, has offered a generous gift of $500,000 to the college, with the stipulation that a diverse panel of student leaders determine the best use of the money "to promote the academic quality of the institution." Pickens also has stipulated that the following constituencies be represented on the panel:

1. Ethnic studies
2. Women's studies
3. Honors Program
4. Student Art Association
5. Young Republicans and Young Democrats
6. Greek organizations
7. Student government
8. Student athletes
9. Students with disabilities
10. Gay/Lesbian/Bisexual Alliance

Pickens believes that the impact of the gift would be dissipated if it were divided among several programs. Therefore, he has stipulated that the money will go to one of the programs represented by the panel members, which the panel is to select by a simple majority vote. If a majority cannot agree on a suitable program within three weeks of the initial meeting, the offer will be withdrawn.

At its initial meeting, the panel agrees to elect Maja, the Honors Program representative, as chair. Thereafter, the spirit of harmony vanishes, and the meeting turns into a catfight. Everyone wants the money for his or her program, and no one seems willing to listen to anyone else.

Maja doesn't want to lose the money, which the college needs badly. Is there anything she can do before the next meeting to end the squabbling and lead the group to consensus?

QUESTIONS TO GUIDE DISCUSSION

1. What are some effective, time-tested strategies for resolving conflict? What strategies have worked for you in the past? Is it easier to resolve a conflict between two parties than among ten? Why or why not? What motivates people to persist in conflict or to yield to compromise? How can Maja motivate the panel members to set aside their disagreements and work toward a common goal?

2. Would it be possible for the panel to agree to fund the best proposal based on a set of objective criteria? What are the ingredients of a good proposal?

3. Was Pickens naive in thinking a consensus could be reached by competing special-interest groups? Or was it a cynical ploy to make a point? If the latter, would the panel achieve greater unity and make better progress if the members understood the donor's motives?

NOW WHAT IF?

* The donor had stipulated that the money should go to a cause or program not represented by any panel member.

* Pickens had specified who should be on the panel, but he had not ruled out other groups, and other groups had petitioned to be on the panel.

* The donor had specified that the money *not* go to homosexuals, women, or nonwhite students, and such students were explicitly barred from the panel.

CASE IN POINT

With all the hostility and distrust in her group, Maja needs to assert her leadership responsibilities with great care. This group will not be easily controlled or influenced. In his book *Leadership in Organizations*, Gary Yukl highlights behaviors within a group that are not authoritarian or controlling but that nonetheless constitute leadership activity and facilitate consensus. These include the following characteristics:

    ▨   Is friendly and supportive

    ▨   Encourages the sharing of ideas before decisions are made

    ▨   Clarifies what should be done and who should do it

    ▨   Sets group priorities and goals

    ▨   Takes initiative in proposing solutions to problems

    ▨   Serves as the group's representative to other groups

    ▨   Helps resolve conflict

1. What additional behaviors or actions could be added to Yukl's list?
2. Which of these facilitating leadership contributions could assist Maja in her role as group leader?
3. Describe a leadership role you have had where such nondirective behaviors were needed. Were you successful in using those behaviors? Why or why not?

WRITING ASSIGNMENT

You are a panel member representing one of the student constituencies listed in the case. You have been asked to make a brief proposal for the best use of the money and to distribute copies to the panel members. Write a proposal containing the following elements:

1. State the *problem* (the situation analysis) that would be solved by the money.
2. Offer a *plan* (goals, objectives) showing how the money would be used to improve the situation described in #1.
3. Show the *probable success* of the plan (the capability statement)—the track record of your organization and the qualifications of its leaders.
4. Make a *pledge* showing how you will assess the outcomes of your plan.

As an appendix to your proposal, include a *budget* (as detailed as you can make it).

SHOWTIME

The class should vote on which of the ten groups represented on the panel would be the best custodian of the money. The two groups with the highest number of votes face off in the debate described below.

    Eight volunteers—four on each side—participate in a debate. Four students represent one organization, four the other. Each group selects its principal debater, then makes its most persuasive case for being the most worthy recipient of the gift.

The principal debaters sit on chairs facing each other. The seconds stand behind them. Each side is permitted to make an opening statement, a rebuttal, and a closing statement—no more than five minutes each. A second may interrupt at any time by tapping a speaker on the shoulder, replacing him or her in the chair, and continuing the speech. (Seconds may not interrupt the opposition.) By the same token, a speaker who has run out of things to say may tap one of the seconds, who is then obliged to take the chair and continue.

When the speeches conclude, the audience members select a winner by a show of hands and explain why they supported one side or the other.

RESEARCH KIT

Print/On-line Resources

- Guidelines on accepting designated gifts (Development Office)
- Books and articles on group goal setting, decision making, and conflict resolution (see Selected Bibliography)
- Handbook on parliamentary procedure
- Student organization mission statements

Human Resources

- College development officer
- Dean of students
- Communications instructor specializing in conflict resolution or group communication
- Leaders of student organizations
- Honors Program director
- Student body president

Selected Bibliography

This bibliography contains an alphabetized listing of reference works, books, and articles related to leadership studies, case learning, conflict resolution, small-group discussion, team building, and critical thinking, as well as a selection of useful World Wide Web sites and electronic discussion groups. Entries have been selected on the basis of their practical value in case learning and leadership training.

Leadership Studies[1]

Reference Works

*Bass, B. M. *Bass and Stogdill's Handbook of Leadership: Theory, Research, and Managerial Applications.* 3rd ed. New York: The Free Press, 1990.

Chemers, M. M., and R. Ayman, eds. *Leadership Theory and Research: Perspectives and Directions.* San Diego: Academic Press, 1993.

Freeman, F. H., K. B. Knott, and M. K. Schwartz. *Leadership Education: A Source Book.* Greensboro, N.C.: Center for Creative Leadership (annual reference work).

Hunt, J. G., B. R. Baliga, H. P. Dachler, and C. A. Schriesheim. *Emerging Leadership Vistas.* Lexington, Mass.: Lexington Books, 1988.

Books

Ambrose, D. *Leadership: The Journey Inward.* Dubuque, Iowa: Kendall/Hunt Publishing, 1991.

Autry, J. *Love and Profit: The Art of Caring Leadership.* New York: William A. Morrow, 1991.

[1]Works identified with an asterisk (*) are cited in the text.

Badaracco, J. L., Jr., and R. R. Ellsworth. *Leadership and the Quest for Integrity.* Boston: Harvard Business School Press, 1989.

Barber, J. D., and B. Kellerman, eds. *Women Leaders in American Politics.* Englewood Cliffs, N.J.: Prentice-Hall, 1986.

Bass, B. M. *Leadership and Performance Beyond Expectations.* New York: The Free Press, 1985.

Bellingham, R., and B. Cohen. *Leadership: Myths and Realities.* Amherst, Mass.: Human Resource Development Press, 1989.

———. *Ethical Leadership: A Competitive Edge.* Amherst, Mass.: Human Resource Development Press, 1990.

Bennis. W. G. *On Becoming a Leader.* Reading, Mass.: Addison-Wesley, 1989.

———. *Why Leaders Can't Lead: The Unconscious Conspiracy Continues.* San Francisco: Jossey-Bass, 1989.

———. *An Invented Life: Reflections on Leadership and Change.* New York: Addison-Wesley, 1993.

Bennis, W. G., and B. Nanus. *Leaders: The Strategies for Taking Charge.* New York: Harper & Row, 1985.

Betz, D. *Cultivating Leadership: An Approach.* Lanham, Md.: University Press of America, 1981.

Birnbaum, R. *How Academic Leadership Works.* San Francisco: Jossey-Bass, 1992.

*Block, P. *Stewardship.* San Francisco: Berrett-Koehler Publishers, 1993.

Bogue, E. G. *The Enemies of Leadership.* Bloomington, Ind.: Phi Delta Kappa, 1985.

Bolman, L. G., and T. E. Deal. *Reframing Organizations: Artistry, Choice, and Leadership.* San Francisco: Jossey-Bass, 1991.

Burns, J. M. *Leadership.* New York: Harper & Row, 1978.

Chaffee, E. E., and W. C. Tierney. *Collegiate Culture and Leadership Strategies.* New York: Macmillan, 1988.

Clark, K. E., and M. B. Clark, eds. *Measures of Leadership.* West Orange, N.J.: Leadership Library of America, 1990.

———. *Choosing to Lead.* Greensboro, N.C.: Leadership Press Ltd., 1994.

Cleary, T., trans. *Zen Lessons: The Art of Leadership.* Boston: Shambahala Publications, 1989.

Clemens, J. K., and D. F. Mayer. *The Classic Touch: Lessons in Leadership from Homer to Hemingway.* Homewood, Ill.: Business One, 1987.

Cleveland, H. *The Knowledge Executive: Leadership in an Information Society.* New York: Dutton, 1985.

Cohen, W. A. *The Art of the Leader.* Englewood Cliffs, N.J.: Prentice-Hall, 1990.

Conger, J. A., et al. *Charismatic Leadership.* San Francisco: Jossey-Bass, 1988.

*Covey, S. R. *The 7 Habits of Highly Effective People.* New York: Simon & Schuster, 1989.

———. *Principle-Centered Leadership.* New York: Summit Books, 1990.

De Pree, M. *Leadership Jazz*. New York: Currency/Doubleday, 1992.

Dinkmeyer, D., and D. Eckstein. *Leadership by Encouragement*. Dubuque, Iowa: Kendall/Hunt, 1993.

DuBrin, A. *Leadership: Research Findings, Practice, and Skills*. Boston: Houghton Mifflin Company, 1995.

Fairholm, G. W. *Values Leadership*. New York: Praeger, 1991.

Gardner, J. W. *Leadership: A Sampler of the Wisdom of John Gardner*. Minneapolis: University of Minnesota, Hubert H. Humphrey Institute, 1981.

*———. *On Leadership*. New York: The Free Press, 1990.

Greenleaf, R. K. *Servant Leadership*. New York: Paulist Press, 1977.

*Hackman, M. Z., and C. E. Johnson. *Leadership: A Communication Perspective*. Prospect Heights, Ill.: Waveland Press, 1991.

Heller, T. *Women and Men as Leaders*. New York: Praeger, 1982.

Hersey, P. *The Situational Leader*. New York: Warner Books, 1984.

Hitt, W. D. *Ethics and Leadership*. Columbus, OH: Batelle Books, 1990.

Hodgkinson, C. *The Philosophy of Leadership*. New York: St. Martin's Press, 1983.

———. *Educational Leadership: The Moral Art*. Albany: State University of New York Press, 1991.

*Hughes, R. L., R. C. Ginnett, and G. J. Curphy. *Leadership: Enhancing the Lessons of Experience*. Homewood, Ill.: Irwin, 1990.

Hunt, J. G. *Leadership: A New Synthesis*. London: Sage, 1991.

Keegan, J. *The Mask of Command*. New York: Penguin, 1988.

Kellerman, B., ed. *Leadership: Multidisciplinary Perspectives*. Englewood Cliffs, N.J.: Prentice-Hall, 1984.

———. *Political Leadership: A Source Book*. Pittsburgh: University of Pittsburgh Press, 1986.

Kelley, R. E. *The Power of Followership*. New York: Doubleday, 1992.

Kets de Vries, M. F. R. *Prisoners of Leadership*. New York: John Wiley & Sons, 1989.

Kokopeli, B., and G. Lakey. *Leadership for Change: Toward a Feminist Model*. Philadelphia: New Society, 1978.

Kouzes, J. M., and B. Z. Posner. *The Leadership Challenge*. San Francisco: Jossey-Boss, 1989.

———. *Credibility: How Leaders Gain and Lose It. Why People Demand It*. San Francisco: Jossey-Bass, 1993.

Losoncy, L. *The Motivating Leader*. Englewood Cliffs, N.J.: Prentice-Hall, 1985.

Manz, C. C., and H. P. Sims, Jr. *Super-Leadership: Leading Others to Lead Themselves*. New York: Berkley Books, 1989.

*McCall, M. W., and M. M. Lombardo. *Off the Track: Why and How Successful Executives Get Derailed*. Greensboro, N.C.: Center for Creative Leadership, 1983.

McCollough, T. E. *The Moral Imagination and Public Life*. Chatham, N.J.: Chatham House Publications, 1991.

McFarland, L. J., L. E. Senn, and J. R. Childress. *21st Century Leadership: Dialogues with 100 Top Leaders.* New York: Leadership Press, 1993.

Nanus, B. *The Leader's Edge: The Seven Keys to Leadership in a Turbulent World.* Chicago: Contemporary Books, 1989.

———. *Visionary Leadership.* San Francisco: Jossey-Bass, 1992.

Peters, T., and N. Austin. *A Passion for Excellence: The Leadership Difference.* New York: Warner Books, 1985.

Rosenbach, W. E., and R. L. Taylor, eds. *Contemporary Issues in Leadership.* Boulder, Colo.: Westview Press, 1993.

Rost, J. *Leadership for the Twenty-First Century.* New York: Praeger, 1991.

Safire, W., and L. Safire, eds. *Leadership.* New York: Simon & Schuster, 1990.

Schein, E. H. *Organizational Culture and Leadership.* 2nd ed. San Francisco: Jossey-Bass, 1992.

Seagren, A. T., et al. *Academic Leadership in the Community Colleges.* Lincoln: University of Nebraska Press, 1994.

Senge, P. *The Fifth Discipline: The Art and Practice of the Learning Organization.* New York: Doubleday, 1990.

Sheehy, G. *Character: America's Search for Leadership.* New York: William A. Morrow, 1988.

Simons, G. F., C. Vasquez, and P. R. Harris. *Transcultural Leadership.* Houston: Gulf Publishing, 1993.

*Smith, P. M. *Taking Charge.* Garden City, N.Y.: Avery Publishing, 1988.

Starratt, R. J. *The Drama of Leadership.* Bristol, Pa.: Falmer Press, 1993.

Stech, E. L. *Leadership Communication.* Chicago: Nelson-Hall, 1983.

Terry, R. W. *Authentic Leadership: Courage in Action.* San Francisco: Jossey-Bass, 1993.

Thompson, K. W., ed. *Essays on Leadership: Comparative Insights.* Lanham, Md.: University Press of America, 1985.

Tichy, N., and M. A. Devanna. *The Transformational Leader.* New York: John Wiley & Sons, 1990.

Toffler, A. *Powershift.* New York: Bantam Books, 1990.

*Utley, R. *The Lance and the Shield.* New York: Ballantine Books, 1993.

*Van Fleet, J. K. *The 22 Biggest Mistakes Managers Make.* West Nyack, N.Y.: Parker, 1973.

Wecter, D. *The Hero in America: A Chronicle of Hero-Worship.* New York: Charles Scribner's Sons, 1972.

Wills, Garry. *Certain Trumpets: The Nature of Leadership.* New York: Simon & Schuster, 1994.

*Yukl, G. A. *Leadership in Organizations.* 2nd ed. Englewood Cliffs, N.J.: Prentice-Hall, 1989.

Zaleznik, A. *Human Dilemmas of Leadership.* New York: Harper & Row, 1966.

Articles

Avolio, B. J., et al. "Leading in the 1990s: The Four I's of Transformational Leadership," *Journal of European Industrial Training*, 15, No. 4 (1991), 9–16.

Bass, B. M. "The Inspirational Processes of Leadership," *Journal of Management Development*, 7, No. 5 (1988), 21–31.

————. "From Transactional to Transformational Leadership: Learning to Share the Vision," *Organizational Dynamics*, 18, No. 3 (1990), 19–31.

Cann, A., and W. D. Siegfried. "Gender Stereotypes and Dimensions of Effective Leader Behavior," *Sex Roles*, 23 (1990), 413–419.

Conger, J. A. "The Dark Side of Leadership," *Organizational Dynamics*, 19, No. 2 (1990), 44–55.

————. "Inspiring Others: The Language of Leadership," *Academy of Management Review*, 5, No. 1 (1991), 31–45.

Covey, S. R. "Leading by Compass," *Executive Excellence*, 8, No. 6 (1991), 3–5.

DeJulio, S. S., et al. "The Measurement of Leadership Potential in College Students," *Journal of College Student Personnel*, 22 (1981), 207–213.

Dobbins, G. H., and S. J. Platz. "Sex Differences in Leadership: How Real Are They?" *Academy of Management Review*, 11 (1986), 118–127.

Drucker, P. F. "Effective Decisions." In *The Effective Executive*. New York: Harper & Row, 1967.

Eagly, A., and S. Korau. "Gender and the Emergence of Leaders," *Psychological Bulletin*, 60, No. 5, (1991), 685–710.

Gardner, J. W. "Leaders and Followers," *Liberal Education*, 73, No. 2 (1987), 4–8.

Gemmill, G., and J. Oakley. "Leadership: An Alienating Social Myth?" *Human Relations*, 45, No. 2 (1992), 113–129.

Hill-Davidson, L. "Black Women's Leadership: Challenges and Strategies," *Signs: Journal of Women in Culture and Society*, 12, No. 2 (1987), 381–385.

Hogan, R., R. Raskin, and D. Fazzini. "How Charisma Cloaks Incompetence," *Personnel Journal*, 69, No. 5 (1990), 73–76.

House, R. J., and J. M. Howell. "Personality and Charismatic Leadership," *Leadership Quarterly*, 3, No. 2 (1992), 81–108.

Howell, J. P., et al. "Substitutes for Leadership: Effective Alternatives to Ineffective Leadership," *Organizational Dynamics*, 19, No. 1 (1990), 21–38.

Kets de Vries, M. F. R. "Leaders Who Self-Destruct: The Causes and Cures," *Organizational Dynamics*, 17, No. 4 (1989), 5–17.

Kiechel, W., III. "The Leader as Servant," *Fortune*, 125, No. 9 (1992), 121–122.

King, A. S. "Evolution of Leadership Theory," *Vikalpa*, 15, No. 2 (1990), 43–54.

Kurzweil, E., et al. "Intellectuals as Leaders," *Partisan Review*, 59, No. 4 (1992), 666–700.

Lee, C. "Followership: The Essence of Leadership," *Training*, 28, No. 1 (1991), 27–35.

Lipman-Blumen, J. "Connective Leadership: Female Leadership Styles in the 21st-Century Workplace," *Sociological Perspectives*, 35, No. 1 (1992), 183–203.

Midgley, M. "Trying Out One's New Sword." In *Heart and Mind*. New York: St. Martin's Press, 1981.

Morgan, G. "Transformational Leadership." In *Creative Organizational Theory*. Newbury Park, Calif.: Sage, 1989.

Mumford, M. D., et al. "Leadership and Destructive Acts: Individual and Situational Influences," *Leadership Quarterly*, 4, No. 2 (1993), 115–147.

Nanus, B. "Visionary Leadership: How to Re-Vision the Future," *Futurist*, 26, No. 5 (1992), 20–25 .

Neville, R. C. "Value, Courage, and Leadership," *Review of Metaphysics*, 43, No. 169 (1989), 3–26.

Rogers, J. L. "New Paradigm Leadership: Integrating the Female Ethos," *Initiatives*, 51, No. 4 (1988), 1–8.

Rosener, J. "Ways Women Lead," *Harvard Business Review*, 68, No. 6 (1990), 119–125.

Schultz, M. C. "Leadership and the Power Circle," *Human Systems Management*, 11, No. 4 (1992), 213–217.

Shoenberg, R. E. "Developing Informed, Effective Campus Leaders," *Chronicle of Higher Education* (September 1993), A68.

Sooklal, L. "The Leader as a Broker of Dreams," *Human Relations*, 44, No. 8 (1991), 833-856.

Wills, G. "What Makes a Good Leader?" *Atlantic Monthly* (April 1994), 63–80.

Teaching and Learning with Cases

Books

Barnes, L., C. R. Christensen, and A. Hanson. *Teaching and the Case Method*. 3rd ed. Boston: Harvard Business School Press, 1994.

Case Writing Group of the Washington Center for Improving the Quality of Undergraduate Education. *Washington Center Casebook on Collaborative Teaching and Learning*. Olympia: Evergreen State College, Washington Center for Improving the Quality of Undergraduate Education, December 1993.

Cragan, J. F., and D. W. Wright. *Communication in Small Group Discussion: A Case Study Approach*. St. Paul: West Publishing, 1980.

Derber, C. *The Pursuit of Attention*. New York: Oxford University Press, 1979.

Education for Judgment: The Artistry of Discussion Leadership. Boston: Harvard Business School Press, 1991.

Erskine, J. A., et al. *Teaching with Cases*. London, Ontario: University of Western Ontario, School of Business Administration, 1981.

Keith-Spiegel, P., A. Wittig, D. V. Perkins, D. W. Balogh, and B. E. Whitley, Jr. *The Ethics of Teaching*. Muncie, Ind.: Ball State University Press, 1993.

Merseth, K. *The Case for Cases in Teacher Education.* Washington, D.C.: American Association for Higher Education and the American Association of Colleges of Teacher Education, 1991.

Meyers, C., and T. Jones. *Promoting Active Learning.* San Francisco: Jossey-Bass, 1993.

Schulman, L. *Case Methods in Teacher Education.* New York: Teachers College Press, 1992.

Schwartz, P., and G. Webb. *Case Study Teaching in Higher Education.* New York: Kogan Page, 1993.

Articles

Argyris, C. "Some Limitations of the Case Method," *Academy of Management Review,* 5 (1980), 291–298.

Berger, M. "In Defense of the Case Method: A Reply to Argyris," *Academy of Management Review,* 5 (1983), 329–333.

Boehrer, J., and M. Linsky. "Teaching with Cases: Learning to Question." In *The Changing Face of College Teaching.* New Directions for Teaching and Learning Series, No. 42 (Summer 1990), 41–57.

Catron, D. "A Case for Cases," *ABCA Bulletin,* 47 (1984), 21–25.

Change (November/December 1993).

DeMichiell, R. L. "Evolution of a Model for Student Case-Writing: From Results to 'Role-Playing.'" In *Case Method Research and Application.* Ed. H. E. Klein. New Vistas. Selected Papers of the Sixth International Case Method Conference (1989), 99–110.

Dezure, D. "Using Cases About Teaching in the Disciplines," *Change,* 25 (November/December 1993), 40–42.

Dezure, D., and W. Shelton. "Promoting a Teaching Culture in Higher Education," *Thought and Action,* 8 (Winter 1993), 27–48.

Grossman, R. W. "Encouraging Critical Thinking Using the Case Study Method and Cooperative Learning Techniques," *Journal on Excellence in College Teaching,* 5, No. 1 (1994), 7–20.

Hawthorne, E. "Case Study and Critical Thinking," *Inquiry,* 41 (1957), 26–27.

Hutchings, P. "Using Cases to Improve College Teaching." Monograph, American Association for Higher Education, Washington, D.C., 1993.

Kingsley, L. "The Case Method as a Form of Communication," *Journal of Business Communication,* 19 (1982), 38–45.

Kleinfeld, J. "What Student Teachers Learn from Writing Cases." Paper presented at the Annual Meeting of the American Educational Research Association, Chicago, April 1991.

Millis, B. "Conducting Cooperative Cases," *To Improve the Academy,* No. 13 (1994), 309–319.

Miner, F. C. "An Approach for Increasing Participation in Case Discussions," *Exchange,* 3 (1978), 41–42.

Reynolds, J. I. "There Is Method in Cases," *Academy of Management Review*, 3 (1978), 129–133.

Schulman, J., J. A. Colbert, D. Kemper, and L. Dmytriew. "Case Writing as a Site for Collaboration," *Teacher Education Quarterly* (Winter 1990), 63–78.

Silverman, R., and W. Welty, "Teaching with Cases," *Journal on Excellence in College Teaching*, 1 (1990), 88–97.

*Sumner, M. "Ethics Online," *Educom Review* (July-August 1996), 32–35.

Tedlock, D. "The Case Approach to Composition," *College Composition and Communication*, 32 (1981), 253–261.

Watson, C. E. "The Case-Study Method and Learning Effectiveness," *College Student Journal*, 9 (1975), 109–116.

Welty, W. "Discussion Method Teaching: A Practical Guide," *To Improve the Academy*, No. 8 (1990), 197–216.

Conflict Resolution

Books

Breslin, J. W., and J. Z. Rubin. *Negotiation Theory and Practice*. Cambridge, Mass.: Program in Negotiation, 1991.

Condlifee, P. *Conflict Management: A Practical Guide*. Collingwood, New Zealand: TAFE, 1991.

Dana, D. *Managing Differences*. Wolcott, Conn.: MTI, 1989.

Deutsch, M. *The Resolution of Conflict*. New Haven: Yale University Press, 1973.

Fisher, R., and W. Ury. *Getting to Yes: Negotiating Agreement Without Giving In*. New York: Penguin, 1983.

Hocker, J. L., and W. W. Wilmot. *Interpersonal Conflict*. 3rd ed. Dubuque, Iowa: Wm. C. Brown, 1991.

Kahn, S. D. *Peacemaking: A Systems Approach to Conflict Management*. Lanham, Md.: University Press of America, 1988.

Katz, N. H., and J. W. Lawyer. *Communication and Conflict Resolution Skills*. Dubuque, Iowa: Kendall/Hunt, 1985.

———. *Conflict Resolution: Building Bridges*. Thousand Oaks, Calif.: Corwin Press, 1993.

———. *Resolving Conflict Successfully: Needed Knowledge and Skills*. Thousand Oaks, Calif.: Corwin Press, 1994.

Pruitt, D. G., and J. Z. Rubin. *Social Conflict: Escalation, Stalemate, and Settlement*. New York: Random House, 1986.

Ury, W. *Getting Past No: Negotiating Your Way from Confrontation to Cooperation*. New York: Bantam, 1993.

Walton, R. E. *Managing Conflict: Interpersonal Dialogue and Third-Party Roles*. 2nd ed. Reading, Mass.: Addison-Wesley, 1987.

Weeks, D. *The Eight Essential Steps to Conflict Resolution*. Los Angeles: Tarcher, 1992.

Articles

Harvey, J. "The Management of Agreement." In *The Abilene Paradox and Other Meditations on Management.* Lexington, Mass.: Lexington Books, 1980.

Katz, N. H., and J. W. Lawyer. "Communication and Conflict Management Skills: Strategies for Individuals and Systems Change," *National Forum*, 63, No. 4 (1983).

Kormanski, C. "Leadership Strategies for Managing Conflict," *Journal for Specialists in Group Work*, 7 (1982), 112–118.

Group Discussion and Team Building

Books

Beebe, S. A., et al. *Communicating in Small Groups: Principles and Practices.* 3rd ed. New York: HarperCollins, 1989.

*Berko, R. M., A. D. Wolvin, and D. R. Wolvin. *Communicating.* New York: Houghton Mifflin Company, 1995.

Bormann, E. G. *Discussion and Group Methods.* 2nd ed. New York: Harper & Row, 1975.

Bouton, C., and R. Y. Garth, eds. *Learning in Groups: New Directions for Teaching and Learning* (No. 14). San Francisco: Jossey-Bass, 1983.

Brilhart, J. K. *Effective Group Discussion.* 4th ed. Dubuque, Iowa: Wm. C. Brown, 1982.

Bruffee, K. A. *Collaborative Learning.* Baltimore: Johns Hopkins University Press, 1993.

Christensen, C. R., et al. *Education for Judgment: The Artistry of Discussion Leadership.* Boston: Harvard Business School Press, 1991.

Fisher, B. A. *Small Group Decision Making.* 2nd ed. New York: McGraw-Hill, 1980.

Forsyth, D. *Group Dynamics.* Pacific Cove, Calif.: Brooks/Cole, 1990.

Goodsell, A., M. Maher, and V. Tinto. *Collaborative Learning: A Sourcebook for Higher Education.* University Park, Pa.: National Center on Postsecondary Teaching, Learning, and Assessment, 1992.

Hackman, R., ed. *Groups That Work (And Those That Don't).* San Francisco: Jossey-Bass, 1990.

Hendrick, C., ed. *Group Processes.* Beverly Hills, Calif.: Sage, 1987.

Hyman, R. T. *Strategic Questioning.* Englewood Cliffs, N.J.: Prentice-Hall, 1979.

Johnson, D. W., and F. P. Johnson. *Joining Together: Group Theory and Group Skills.* 4th ed. Englewood Cliffs, N.J.: Prentice-Hall, 1991.

Katzenbach, J. R., and D. R. Smith. *The Wisdom of Teams.* New York: HarperCollins, 1994.

*Larson, C. E., and F. LaFasto. *Teamwork.* Newbury Park, Calif.: Sage, 1989.

Napier, R. W., and M. K. Gershenfeld. *Making Groups Work: A Guide for Group Leaders.* Boston: Houghton Mifflin Company, 1983.

Nyaman, R. T. *Improving Discussion Leadership.* New York: Teachers College Press, 1980.

Patton, B. P., K. Giffin, and E. N. Patton. *Decision-Making Group Interaction.* 3rd ed. New York: Harper & Row, 1989.

Wilson, G. L., and M. S. Hanna. *Groups in Context: Leadership and Participation in Small Groups.* New York: Random House, 1986.

Articles

Dobbins, G., and S. Zaccaro. "The Effects of Group Cohesion and Leader Behavior on Subordinate Satisfaction," *Group and Organization Studies,* 11, No. 3 (1986), 203–219.

Dukerich, J., et al. "Moral Reasoning in Groups," *Human Relations,* 43, No. 5 (1990), 473–493.

Eskilson, A., and M. Wiley. "Sex Composition and Leadership in Small Groups," *Sociometry,* 39, No. 3 (1976), 183–194.

Feichtner, S. B., and E. A. Davis. "Why Some Groups Fail: A Survey of Students' Experiences with Learning Groups," *Organizational Behavior Teaching Review,* No. 9 (1985), 58–73.

Frederick, P. "The Dreaded Discussion: Ten Ways to Start," *Improving College and University Teaching,* 29 (1981), 109–114.

Gadlen, H., and R. Rosenwein. "Process Issues in the Discussion Group," *Improving College and University Teaching,* 16 (1968), 250–257.

Gist, M., E. Locke, and S. Taylor. "Group Structure, Process and Effectiveness," *Journal of Management,* (1987), 237–257.

Hirschhorn, L. "Introducing and Facilitating the Team Process." In *Managing in the New Team Environment.* Reading, Mass.: Addison-Wesley, 1991.

Kolb, J. A. "Leadership of Creative Teams," *Journal of Creative Behavior,* 26, No. 1 (1992), 1–9.

Schein, E. H. "The Structure and Function of Groups." In *Organizational Psychology.* 3rd ed. Englewood Cliffs, N.J.: Prentice-Hall, 1980.

Whyte, G. "Groupthink Reconsidered," *Academy of Management Review,* 14, No. 1 (1989), 40–56.

Critical Thinking

Books

Anderson, W. *Diderot's Dream.* Baltimore: Johns Hopkins University Press, 1990.

Brookfield, S. *Developing Critical Thinkers: Challenging Adults to Explore Alternative Ways of Thinking and Acting.* San Francisco: Jossey-Bass, 1986.

Chaffee, J. *The Thinker's Guide to College Success.* Boston: Houghton Mifflin Company, 1996.

Critical Thinking: Educational Imperative. San Francisco: Jossey-Bass, 1992.

Heiman, M. *Critical Thinking Skills.* Washington, D.C.: National Education Association, 1985.

Hitchcock, D. *Critical Thinking.* Toronto: Methuen, 1983.

Kurfiss, J. G. *Critical Thinking: Theory, Research, Practice, and Possibilities. ASHE-ERIC Higher Education Report No. 2.* Washington, D.C.: Association for the Study of Higher Education, 1988.

McPeck, J. E. *Teaching Critical Thinking: Dialogue and Dialectic.* New York: Routledge, 1990.

Meyers, C. *Teaching Students to Think Critically.* San Francisco: Jossey-Bass, 1986.

Moore, B. N., and R. Parker. *Critical Thinking.* Mountain View, Calif.: Mayfield, 1986.

Paul, R. *Critical Thinking: What Every Person Needs to Survive in a Rapidly Changing World.* Santa Rosa, Calif.: Foundation for Critical Thinking, 1990.

————. *Critical Thinking: How to Prepare Students for a Rapidly Changing World.* Santa Rosa, Calif.: Foundation for Critical Thinking, 1993.

Regal, P. J. *The Anatomy of Judgment.* Minneapolis: University of Minnesota Press, 1989.

Resnick, L. B. *Education and Learning to Think.* Washington, D.C.: National Academy Press, 1987.

Ruggiero, V. R. *Becoming a Critical Thinker.* 2nd ed. Boston: Houghton Mifflin Company, 1996.

Siegel, H. *Educating Reason: Rationality, Critical Thinking, and Education.* New York: Routledge, 1988.

Walters, K. S., ed. *Re-Thinking Reason: New Perspectives in Critical Thinking.* New York: State University of New York Press, 1995.

Warnick, B. *Critical Thinking and Communication: The Use of Reason in Argument.* New York: Macmillan, 1986.

Articles

Caberera, G. A. "Reading Critically About Critical Thinking: Recommended Sources," *Journal of Reading,* 37 (February 1994), 423–433.

Ennis, R. H. "Critical Thinking: What Is It?" In *Philosophy of Education.* Ed. H. A. Alexander. Urbana, Ill.: Philosophy of Education Society, 1992.

Evans, M. D. "Using Classroom Debates as a Learning Tool," *Social Education,* 57 (November 1993), 370.

Howie, S. H. "Critical Thinking: A Critical Skill for Students." *Reading Today,* 10 (April 1993), 25.

Johnson, D. W. "Creative and Critical Thinking Through Academic Controversy," *American Behavioral Scientist,* 37 (September 1993), 40–53.

Lewis, J. "Redefining Critical Reading for College Critical Thinking Courses," *Journal of Reading,* 34 (March 1991), 420–423.

Lown, J. M. "Teaching Issue Analysis and Critical Thinking Through Role Playing," *Journal of Education for Business,* 62 (October 1987), 20–23.

MacDonald, S. C. "Critical Thinking: Grokking the Fullness," *College Teaching*, 36 (Summer 1987), 91–93.

McMillan, J. H. "Enhancing College Students' Critical Thinking: A Review of Studies," *Research in Higher Education*, 26, No.1 (1987), 3–29.

Menssen, S. "Critical Thinking and the Construction of Knowledge," *American Behavioral Scientist*, 37 (September 1993), 85–93.

Paul, R. W. "The Logic of Creative and Critical Thinking," *American Behavioral Scientist*, 37 (September 1993), 21–39.

Paul, R. W., and J. Rudinow. "Bias, Relativism, and Critical Thinking," *Journal of Thought*, 23 (Fall/Winter 1987), 125–133.

van Allen, L. "Musings on Critical Thinking," *English Journal*, 84 (November 1994), 108–109.

Useful Internet Resources

World Wide Web (WWW) Sites

College and Universities
http://www.utexas.edu/world/univ/state/
Links to central servers of U.S. higher education institutions, organized by state.

Discussion Groups (Listservs)
http://www.nova.edu/Inter-Links/listserv.html
The Inter-Links Mailing List Locator, an encyclopedic directory of electronic discussion groups on every conceivable topic.

Education (General)
http://ericir.syr.edu/
Accesses the AskERIC Home Page, with links to a vast bibliography of educational resources.

Leadership
http://www.cdinet.com/millennium/Resource/leader.html
Useful list of leadership organizations in the United States, with names and addresses of contact persons.

http://www.ccl.org/frontpage/frontpage/
The Center for Creative Leadership, based in Greensboro, N.C., provides organizations with leadership training, consulting, publications, and support services.

Legal Information
http://www.lawsites.com
A comprehensive, searchable site for legal information.

Legislation (Federal)
http://thomas.loc.gov/
Legislative information, including historical documents such as the U.S. Constitution and *The Federalist Papers*.

Search Engines (Web Site Locators)
http://www.altavista.digital.com/
This site, Alta Vista, is the largest WWW search engine but there are many other good ones, including Excite, HotBot, WebCrawler Searching, and Yahoo!. Use any words to search for sites on any topic.

Student Affairs
http://www.ucc.uconn.edu/~wwwwdosa
Various discussion groups for student affairs professionals and student leaders.

U.S. Government Agencies
http://www.eit.com/web/www.servers/government.html
Links to federal agencies.

Women and Leadership
http://www.cowan.edu.au/dvc/irwl/welcome.htm
Home page of the *International Review of Women and Leadership*, published by Edith Cowan University in Perth, Western Australia.